BIG
ENGLISH 2
PLUS

Mario Herrera • Christopher Sol Cruz

STUDENT'S BOOK

Contents

Unit	Vocabulary	Structures
1 In My Classroom pp. 4–19	**Classroom activities:** coloring, counting, cutting, gluing, listening, playing a game, using the computer, watching a DVD, writing	What's he doing? He's using the computer. How many pictures are there? There's one picture./There are three pictures. Be careful. Don't be silly. Listen to me. Don't eat in the classroom.
2 My Games pp. 20–35	**Activities:** climbing trees, doing gymnastics, flying kites, ice-skating, playing tennis, playing volleyball, riding my bike, skateboarding	What do you like doing? I like playing tennis. What does she love doing? She loves skating. They love to swim. Me, too! She doesn't like to play. Me neither!
3 In My House pp. 36–51	**Furniture:** bathtub, bed, chair, closet, couch, dresser, DVD player, fridge, lamp, oven, sink, table, TV **Prepositions:** behind, between, in front of, next to **Rooms:** bathroom, bedroom, dining room, kitchen, living room **Family:** aunt, cousin, uncle	Where's the TV? It's on the table. Ben's keys are on the table. She has a bag. The bag is hers.
Checkpoint Units 1–3 pp. 52–55	**Units 1–3 Exam Preparation** pp. 56–57	
4 In My Town pp. 58–73	**Places:** bank, book store, bus stop, computer store, gas station, movie theater, post office, restaurant, shopping mall, supermarket, train station **Verbs:** buy, send	We want to buy a book. He wants to go to the post office. Is there a bank on Elm Street? Yes, there is./No, there isn't. How much is it? It's two dollars and ten cents.
5 My Dream Job pp. 74–89	**Jobs:** actor, artist, athlete, chef, dancer, doctor, pilot, singer, teacher, vet, writer	What do you want to be? I want to be an actor. What does she want to be? She wants to be a doctor. Tim wants to be a doctor because he loves science. You look tired. Are you OK?
6 My Day pp. 90–105	**Clock times:** one o'clock, two o'clock, three o'clock, four o'clock, five o'clock, six o'clock, seven o'clock, eight o'clock, nine o'clock, ten o'clock, eleven o'clock, twelve o'clock **Verbs:** finish, get up, go out, go to bed, start, watch TV	When does he get up? He gets up at six o'clock. Who are you? What's your job? Where do you work? How many students are there?
Checkpoint Units 4–6 pp. 106–109	**Units 4–6 Exam Preparation** pp. 110–111	
7 My Favorite Food pp. 112–127	**Food:** apples, bananas, burgers, carrots, cheese, mangoes, meat, oranges, potatoes, sandwiches, snack, strawberries, tomatoes, vegetables, yogurt	Do you like fruit? Yes, I do. I like apples. No, we don't. We don't like fruit. I want an apple and some pears. He has some water.
8 Wild Animals pp. 128–143	**Animals:** cheetah, crocodile, elephant, giraffe, hippo, kangaroo, monkey, parrot, peacock, polar bear, snake, zebra **Verbs:** chase, climb trees	Can a kangaroo jump? Yes, it can. Can snakes run? No, they can't. A big new camera.
9 Fun All Year pp. 144–159	**Months of the year:** January, February, March, April, May, June, July, August, September, October, November, December **Adverbs of frequency:** always, never	What does he do in January? He always has a New Year's party in January. Do you go on vacation in the winter? No, we don't. We never go on vacation in the winter. It's cold. It's snowing.
Checkpoint Units 7–9 pp. 160–163	**Units 7–9 Exam Preparation** pp. 164–165	

Young Learners English Practice Starters pp. 166–175   Wordlist pp. 176–179   Big English Song p. 180   Cutouts pp. 181–185

CLIL/Culture	Values	Phonics	I can...
Math: Arithmetic numbers 11–100, plus, minus, equals 10 minus 6 equals... / 5 plus 5 equals... **Around the World: Classes** in a forest/garden, in the mountains, on a boat	**Take turns.** May I use the computer now? Yes! Let's take turns.	**th** that, the, then, this, with bath, both, math, mouth, path, thin	...talk about what people are doing in the classroom. ...count to 100. ...talk about taking turns.
Science: Bones and muscles bones, exercise, jump, kick, move, muscle, strong, throw, weak We throw with our hands. When we jump, we use ... muscles. **Around the World: Games**	**Play safely.** safe, seesaw, skateboard, slide, swing I want to play on the slide. Always slide with your feet in front of you.	**ng, nk** bang, king, ring, sing, wing bank, ink, pink, sink, thank	...say what people like doing/to do. ...talk about how my body works. ...talk about playing safely.
History: Old and new things burn, museum, new, oil, old, screen, wheel This is an old phone. / This phone is old. **Around the World: Household objects** clay, comfortable, dry, electricity, fuel, hammock, household, solar, wet	**Be neat.** sink, toy box, washing machine	**oo** cool, food, moon, room, zoo book, cook, foot, good, look	...say where things are. ...talk about possessions. ...talk about new and old objects.
Geography: Transportation around the world boat, canal, fast, ground, safe, slow, subway In Bangkok, many students go to school by boat. **Around the World: Taxis** design, famous, long time ago, sign	**Cross the street safely.** cross, first, left, pedestrian crossing, right, wait	**ai, oa** nail, rain, tail, train, wait boat, coat, oak, road, soap	...say what I want and talk about money. ...describe where places are in town. ...talk about different kinds of transportation.
Social Science: Goods and services carpenter, entertain, farmer, hairdresser, nurse, produce, provide, take care of, waiter A nurse helps sick people. **Around the World: Jobs** park ranger, protect, rodeo rider, scuba dive	**Study hard and set goals.** art, math, music, science	**ar, er, or** arm, art, car, cart letter, singer, teacher born, corn, for	...talk about jobs. ...say what I want to be and why. ...talk about studying hard and setting goals.
History: Telling the time burn, candle, cup, fall, height, hourglass, sand, shadow, sundial We use clocks to tell time. **Around the World: Routines** after/before school, (at) recess, tired	**Be on time.** I get my backpack ready the night before school. I get up early on school days. I get dressed quickly and eat breakfast. I always get to school on time.	**ch, tch, sh** chin, chop, lunch, rich match, watch, witch dish, fish, ship, she	...talk about times and daily activities. ...ask questions. ...talk about different ways of telling time.
Science: Healthy and unhealthy snacks diabetes, disease, fat, healthy, heart, label, salt, sugar, too much, unhealthy **Around the World: Fruit** avocado, chocolate, fabric, kiwi, leaves, pineapple, popular, round, square, tropical, watermelon	**Choose healthy foods.** apple, cookie, carrots, chips No chips for me, thanks. Just one cookie, please.	**ee, ie** bee, cheese, feet, see, sheep cried, flies, lie, pie, tie	...talk about food. ...talk about healthy and unhealthy food. ...say where fruit comes from.
Science: Animal habitats cover, desert, fox, jungle, lizard, ocean, raccoon, seal, whale Lizards live in deserts. **Around the World: Outside my window** gum tree, interesting, koala, llama, snowball, website, wonderful	**Appreciate animals.** amazing, beautiful, smart, strong	**ou, ow** group, soup, toucan, you clown, cow, down, owl, town	...describe animals. ...talk about where animals live. ...talk about appreciating animals.
Geography: Seasonal festivals celebration, confetti, hang, pole, wish In England, people celebrate May Day. May Day is in the spring. **Around the World: New Year's Eve** chime, coal, fireworks, good luck, grapes, midnight, noodle soup, ring	**Be active all year.** fall, spring, summer, winter rake leaves, ride bikes, ice-skate, swim	**Alphabet**	...talk about what I do each month. ...talk about the weather. ...talk about seasonal holidays.

unit 1

In My Classroom

2

1 Listen, look, and say.

1 coloring

2 counting

3 cutting

4 gluing

5 listening

6 watching a DVD

7 using the computer

8 writing

9 playing a game

3

2 Listen, find, and say.   **3** Play a game.

4 Listen and sing. Then look at **1** and find.

Here's My Classroom!

Look! Here's my classroom.
And here are my friends!
Peter, Sarah, and Timothy,
Penny, Jack, and Jen!

Peter is cutting paper.
Penny is writing her name.
Sarah is listening to a story,
And Jack is playing a game.

Timothy is counting.
Jen is gluing.
We have fun and learn a lot.
What are your friends doing?

5 Listen and find in **1**. Then say.

6 Look at **1**. Ask and answer.

What's she doing?

She's coloring.

THINK BIG What can we write?
What can we count?

7 Listen and read. How many Marias are there?

8 Look at the story. Then match.

1 She's cutting paper.

2 She's gluing pictures.

3 She's using the computer.

4 She's writing on the board.

a

b

THINK BIG Are there any girls called Maria in your class? How many?
How many children are there with the same name? What are the names?

9 Listen. Help Jamie and Jenny make sentences.

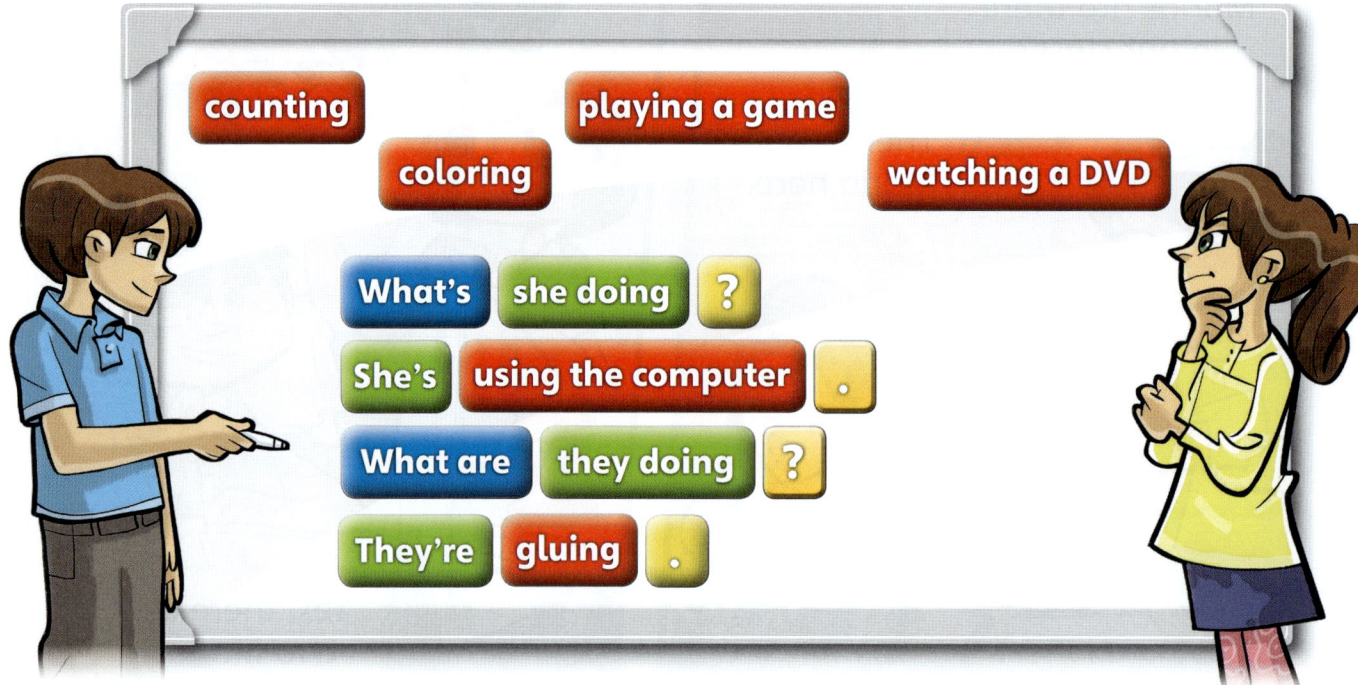

counting
playing a game
coloring
watching a DVD

What's | she doing | ?
She's | using the computer | .
What are | they doing | ?
They're | gluing | .

10 Look and write.

1 What's he _____?
He's _____ his name.

2 What's she _____?
_____ a picture.

3 _____ they _____?
_____ to a story.

4 _____?
_____ paper.

11 **Listen and stick. Then say.** 12

12 **Look at 11. Ask and answer. Use How many.**

How many computers are there?

There are two computers.

13 **Draw and write. Use There's or There are.**

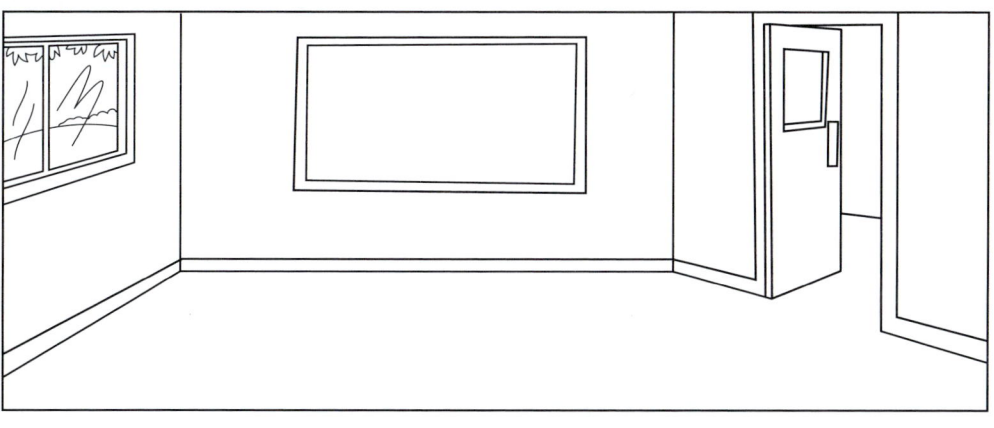

_____

_____

14 **Do the math. Then listen.**

1 Four plus three equals _____.

2 Eight minus two equals _____.

3 One plus nine equals _____.

> **CONTENT WORDS**
> plus +
> minus −
> equals =

 15 **Look, listen, and read. Then match and write a–e.**

> **CONTENT WORDS**
> eleven 11   twelve 12   thirteen 13   fourteen 14   fifteen 15   sixteen 16
> seventeen 17   eighteen 18   nineteen 19   twenty 20   thirty 30   forty 40
> fifty 50   sixty 60   seventy 70   eighty 80   ninety 90   a hundred 100

Math Homework   Katie Timms

1   There are eleven girls in the class and nineteen boys.
There are __*thirty*__ children in the class. ☐

2   There are fourteen chairs in Classroom 1. The children
move thirteen of them to Classroom 2. Now there are
__*fifty*__ chairs in Classroom 1. ☐

3   The children have fifteen cupcakes. They eat four. Now
they have __*twelve*__ cupcakes. ☐

4   There are eighteen pictures on the paper. Lucy cuts out
sixteen pictures. Now there are __*two*__ pictures on the
paper. ☐

5   There are a hundred children on the playground. Forty
go into their classrooms. Now there are __*seventy*__ children
on the playground. ☐

a $14 - 13 = 50$ ✗   b $100 - 40 = 70$ ✗

c $11 + 19 = 30$ ✓   d $15 - 4 = 12$ ✗

e $18 - 16 = 2$ ✓

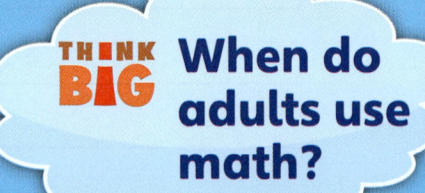

THINK BIG When do adults use math?

16 Listen and circle. Then ask and answer.

1 **17** / **70**   2 **59** / **95**

3 **69** / **89**   4 **31** / **33**

5 **47** / **27**   6 **23** / **22**

> What's this?

> Sixty-nine!

17 Count and write, then listen. Then say and answer.

1 $30 + 40 =$ ☐   2 $20 - 2 =$ ☐

3 $60 - 10 =$ ☐   4 $11 + 1 =$ ☐

5 $80 + 4 =$ ☐   6 $19 - 6 =$ ☐

7 $17 - 3 =$ ☐   8 $95 + 5 =$ ☐

> Thirty plus forty equals…

> Seventy!

PROJECT

18 Make a Math poster. Then present it to the class.

$$12 \quad + \quad 3 \quad = \quad 15$$

Twelve plus three equals fifteen.

> Here are twelve pens. Here are three pens. There are fifteen pens. Twelve plus three equals fifteen.

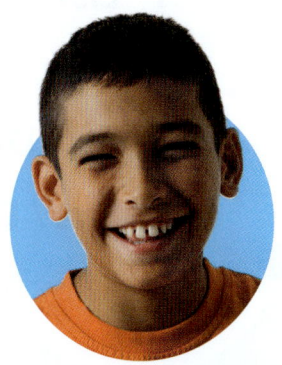

19 **Listen and read. Then say.**

Mrs. Green: It's hot in the classroom. Open the window, please, Lucy.

Lucy: OK.

Mrs. Green: Don't stand on the table. There's a computer on it! Be careful!

Lucy: Can I stand on the computer?

Mrs. Green: Don't be silly! Stand on the chair, open the window, and then sit down. And be quick, please, Lucy.

20 **Read. Then circle Don't in 19.**

Stand on the chair.	**Don't stand** on the table.
Be careful.	**Don't be** silly.

Stand on the chair. ✔
You stand on the chair. ✘

Be careful! ✔
Are careful! ✘

Don't (= Do not) stand on the table. ✔
Don't be silly. ✔

21 **Read and circle.**

Class Rules

1 **Listen / Don't listen** to the teacher.

2 **Talk / Don't talk** when the teacher is talking.

3 **Be / Don't be** careful when you're cutting paper.

4 **Eat / Don't eat** food in the classroom.

22 **Put the words in order. Then say.**

1 quick. Be

2 picture. Color the

3 use Don't computer. the

4 a Play game.

23 **Look and write.**

1 write ✓ throw ✗
_____ on the paper,
please. _____
_____ it.

2 talk ✗ listen ✓
_____ _____ to
your friend. _____ to
the teacher.

3 be ✗ dry ✓
_____ _____ sad.
_____ your eyes.

4 wake up ✓ be ✗
_____ _____, Jenny!
_____ _____ late!

Classes, but Not in a Classroom!

Are classes always in classrooms? No, they aren't!

a

These students in Turkey aren't in their classroom today. They're in a forest. They're studying trees and animals.

These students live in the mountains in France. They're having a P.E. class. It's very cold, but they're having fun. They love to ski.

b

24 **Look at the pictures. Where are the children?**

in a forest   in a garden   in the mountains   on a boat

19

25 **Listen and read. Then match and write a–d.**

They're doing/studying: **1** P.E. ☐   **2** science ☐

3 animals ☐   **4** English ☐

26 **Look at 25. Read and circle.**

1 It's **hot / cold** in the mountains in France.

2 The students in France are **skiing / climbing**.

3 There **is / isn't** a garden at the school in the United States.

4 The boat school is **always / sometimes** open.

These students in the United States are having a science class in the school garden. They're growing plants and flowers.

d

These students are studying English in a classroom in Bangladesh. Their school is a boat! Bangladesh is a wet country. Sometimes schools close, but this school is always open.

c

27 **Talk about your classroom with a friend.**

Our classroom is in Mexico. There are twenty desks and chairs.

We have a big whiteboard and six new computers.

THINK BIG **Do you have classes outside the classroom? Where do you go? What do you study?**

21
28 **Listen and look. Number in order.**

a  b  c

29 **Take turns. Ask and answer. Do the actions.**

May I use the computer now?

Yes! Let's take turns.

THINK BIG **Is it good to take turns? Why?**

22
30 **Listen, look, and repeat.**

1 th   **2** th

23
31 **Listen and find. Then say.**

ba**th**   **th**in

this   **th**at

24
32 **Listen and blend the sounds.**

1 th-e   the   **2** th-e-n   then
3 b-o-th   both   **4** w-i-th   with
5 p-a-th   path   **6** m-a-th   math

25
33 **Underline th and th. Then listen and chant.**

There are three crocodiles
Taking a bath.
They have thin mouths,
But big teeth!
Look out! Look out!

34 **Listen and find. Say Picture 1 or Picture 2. Then ask and answer.**

Picture 1

Picture 2

In Picture 1, what are they doing?

In Picture 1, they're playing a game.
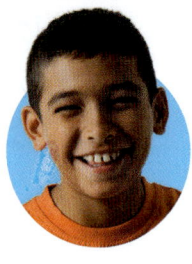

35 **Look and write rules.**

1 _____ to the teacher. ✓

2 _____ your name on your notebook. ✓

3 _____ _____ to music. ✗

4 _____ _____ DVDs. ✗

36 **Count and write. Use There's or There are.**

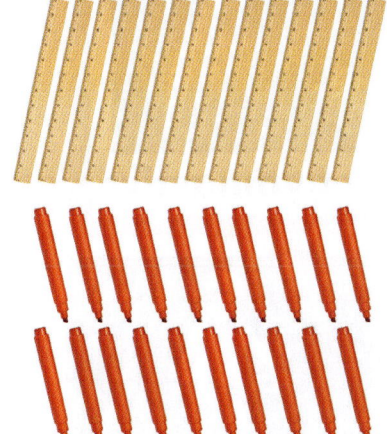

1 _____ _____ rulers.

2 _____ _____ an eraser.

3 _____ _____ markers.

I Can

☐ talk about what people are doing in the classroom.

☐ count to 100.

☐ talk about taking turns.

My Games

28
1 **Listen, look, and say.**

1 flying kites

2 playing volleyball

3 playing tennis

4 climbing trees

5 doing gymnastics

6 ice-skating

7 skateboarding

8 riding my bike

29
2 **Listen, find, and say.** **3** **Play a game.**

4 Listen and sing. Then look at 1 and find.

Come On and Play

We're playing on the playground.
There are a lot of games to play.
Soccer, tennis, and volleyball.
What do you want to play today?

Paul likes playing on the swings.
Emma likes running and climbing.
We all love riding our bikes.
Tell us! What do you like doing?

We're playing on the playground.
It's always so much fun.
Come on and play with us.
We play with everyone!

32

5 Listen and ✔.

a
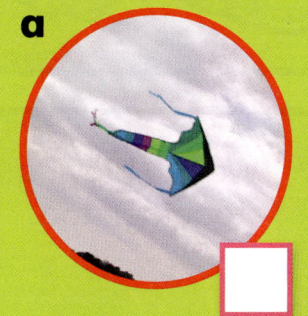

b

c

d

6 Look at 1. Ask and answer.

I like playing volleyball.

Picture 2.

THINK BIG What games can children play in the playground?
What games can children play in the classroom?

7 **Listen and read. What does Jenny like doing?**

8 Look at the story. Then circle.

1  likes **playing soccer / riding his bike**.

2  loves **playing tennis / skateboarding**.

3  likes **playing volleyball / flying kites**.

THINK BIG What do you like playing on the playground?
What team games do you know?
Do you like playing on a team? Why?

9 Listen. Help Jamie and Jenny make sentences.

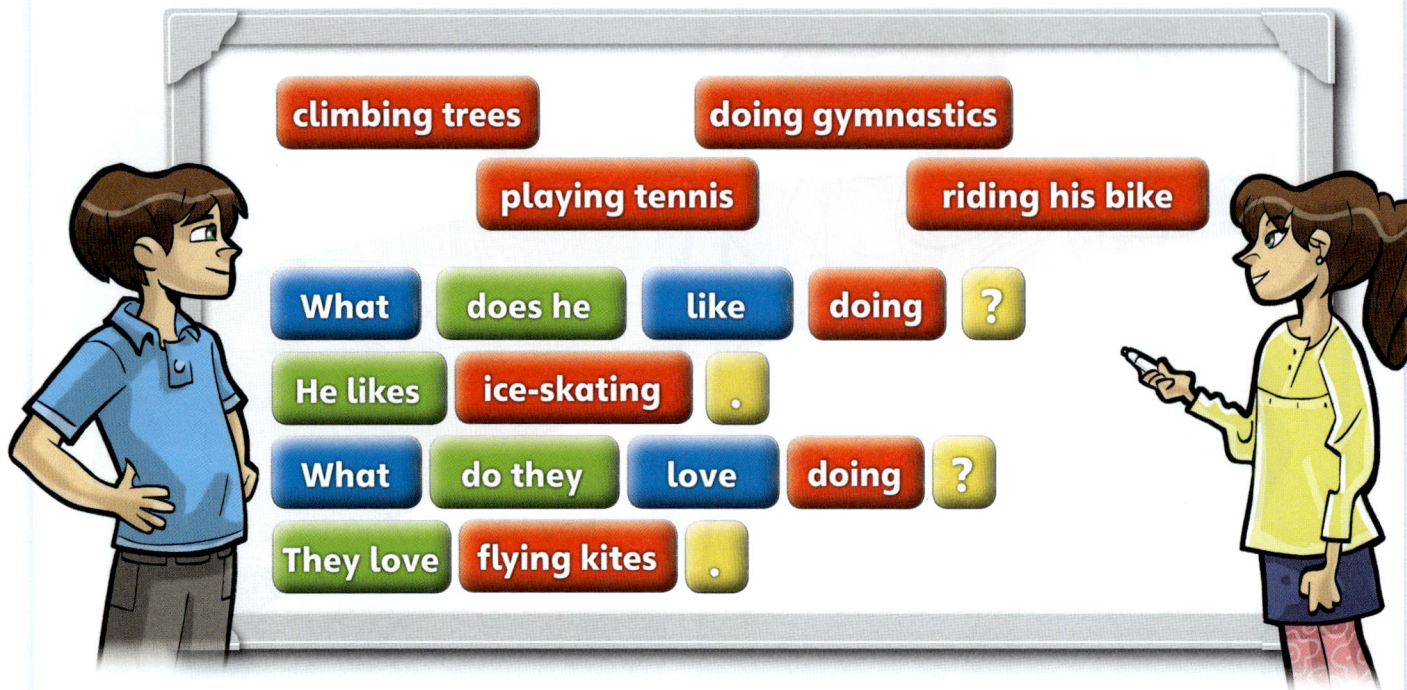

10 Look and write. Use **like** or **love**.

1 What _____ she like doing?
She likes _____.

2 What _____ they love _____?
They _____.

3 _____ you _____?
I _____.

4 _____?
_____.

37
11 Listen and stick. Then say.

12 Look at 11. Ask and answer.

What do they love doing?

They love flying kites.

13 Write and draw.

I love _____
_____
_____
_____.

14 **Look. Circle the body words. How many are there?**

> bones   feet   fingers   help   milk   muscles

15 **Look, listen, and read. Then circle.**
38

> **CONTENT WORDS**
> bone   exercise   jump   kick   move   muscle   strong   throw   weak

Bones and Muscles

a Playing is fun, and our bones and muscles help us play. Our bodies move when our muscles pull our bones into different positions.

b Our hands have a lot of bones. There are [1]**27 / 70** bones in one hand. When we throw a ball with our hands, we use [2]**43 / 34** muscles.

c Our feet have a lot of bones, too. There are [3]**20 / 26** bones in one foot. When we kick a ball with our foot, we use [4]**13 / 30** muscles. When we jump, we use more than [5]**17 / 70** muscles.

d When we exercise every day, we use our muscles, and they grow strong. But when we don't exercise, they grow weak. Milk, yogurt, and cheese help make our bones strong. We need to take good care of our bones and muscles.

Muscle →

Bone →

THINK BIG **Which activities make our muscles strong?**
dancing   using a computer   watching DVDs
playing tennis   climbing trees

16 Look at **15**. Read and match.

1 Bones and muscles   **a** make our bones strong.
2 Our hands   **b** makes our muscles strong.
3 When we throw a ball, we   **c** help us play.
4 When we jump, we   **d** use more than 70 muscles.
5 Exercise   **e** use our hands.
6 Milk and cheese   **f** have a lot of bones.

17 Look, choose and say.

| drink milk   eat yogurt and cheese   exercise |

| bones   muscles   strong   weak |

I exercise every day.

I don't drink milk.

You have strong muscles.

You have weak bones.

PROJECT

18 Make a **Body** poster about an activity. Then present it to the class.

Bones and Muscles in Volleyball

I love volleyball.

There are three bones in an arm and 27 bones in a hand.

In volleyball, we hit the ball with our hands and arms.

When we jump, we use more than 70 muscles.

We hit the ball with our hands and arms.

Grammar

19 🎧 **40 Listen and read. Then say.**

Anna:	Does your sister like to play sports?
Ben:	She doesn't like to play soccer or basketball, but she loves to skateboard.
Anna:	Me, too! It's my favorite sport.
Ben:	What about your brothers? What sports do they like?
Anna:	They like volleyball and tennis, and they love to swim. But they don't like to swim in the ocean.
Ben:	Me neither! It's very cold.

20 **Read. Then circle** don't **and** doesn't **in** **19.**

She loves to skateboard. **They love to** swim.	**Me, too!**
She doesn't like to play soccer. **They don't like to** swim in the ocean.	**Me neither!**

I/you/we/they **like to** play. ✔
He/She/It **likes to** play. ✔
I/You/We/They **don't like to** ice-skate. ✔
He/She/It **doesn't like to** ice-skate. ✔

21 **Read and circle.**

1. I love to climb trees.   **Me, too. / Me neither.**

2. My dad doesn't like to ice-skate.   **Me, too. / Me neither.**

3. My sister doesn't have a skateboard.   **Me, too. / Me neither.**

4. My parents like to ride bikes.   **Me, too. / Me neither.**

22 **Look and say.**

1 They (like ✗) to play hopscotch.
2 He (love ✓) to play on the slide.
3 She (have ✗) a bike.
4 He always (drink ✓) milk for healthy bones.

23 **Write.**

| doesn't | don't | like | loves | neither | too |

A: I love dogs.

B: Me, ¹_____!

A: My dog's name is Billy, and he's very funny. He doesn't
²_____ to eat bones, and he ³_____ like to
catch balls, but he ⁴_____ to skateboard. I don't
understand it!

B: Me ⁵_____, but my dogs are funny, too. They
⁶_____ like to run, but they love to ride on my
mom's bike!

24 **Work with a friend. Look and say.**

Do you like to...	Jim and Tim	Sarah	Alex
fly kites?	✓	✗	✗
do gymnastics?	✓	✓	✗
sing?	✗	✗	✓

Jim and Tim like to fly kites.

Me, too!

Games You Play →

1   I like to play jacks. I play on my own, but you can play with friends, too. You need a small ball and ten jacks. You throw the ball, and you pick up the jacks before you catch the ball again.

Elena, Guatemala

jack

25 **Look at the pictures. Which games do you know? Who do you play with?**

41

26 **Listen and read. Then write Elena, Arnav, or John.**

1 _____ plays with stones.

2 _____ catches a ball.

3 _____ hits something.

27 **Look at 26. Read and match.**

Name	Game	You need	You
Elena	mancala	marbles	hit
Arnav	jacks	jacks and a ball	move and take
John	marbles	stones and a board	throw, pick up, and catch

2   Children in my city like to play marbles after school. A lot of people can play this game together. You hit a marble with your finger. When I win my friends' marbles, I'm very happy.

Arnav, India

board

stone

3   My friends and I like to play mancala. It's a game for two people. You need a board and some stones. You move the stones around the board. It's good when you catch your friend's stones.

John, Ghana

marble

28 **Complete the chart about a game you like. Then ask and answer.**

What's the game?	
What do you need?	
What do you do?	

What's the game?

Hopscotch.

THINK BIG **Which games do you like to play? What do you need for your games?**

43
 **29 Listen and number.**

a

b

c

d

skateboard   swing   seesaw   slide

44
 30 Listen and write. Then say.

feet   hands   knee   leg

A

1 I want to play on the slide.

2 I want to play on the swing.

3 I want to play on the seesaw.

4 I want to skateboard.

B

Always slide with your
_____ in front of you.

Always sit down and hold on
with both _____ .

Always put one _____
on each side.

Always wear a helmet
and _____ pads.

 I want to play on the slide.

Always slide with your feet in front of you.

THINK BIG Do you play safely? How?

45
 31 **Listen, look, and repeat.**

1 ng   **2** nk

46
32 **Listen and find. Then say.**

ri**ng**

ba**ng**

pi**nk**

i**nk**

47
 33 **Listen and blend the sounds.**

1 k-i-ng   king   **2** w-i-ng   wing

3 th-a-nk   thank   **4** s-i-ng   sing

5 b-a-nk   bank   **6** s-i-nk   sink

48
 34 **Underline ng and nk. Then listen and chant.**

Sing a song about a king.
Thank you! Thank you!
He has a big, pink ring
And big, blue wings.
Thank you! Thank you!

35 **Work in groups. Play the Memory game.**

Student 1:
What do you like doing on the playground? Say.

Student 2:
Talk about Student 1. What does she like doing? Then say and act out what you like doing.

I like playing volleyball.

Susan likes playing volleyball. I like riding my bike.

Susan likes playing volleyball. Peter likes riding his bike. I like ice-skating.

Student 3:
Talk about Students 1 and 2. Then say and act out what you like doing.

Play with your group. Can you remember what everyone likes doing?

36 **Look and write. Use like or love.**

1 _____
to fly kites.

2 _____
to play tennis.

3 _____
to play soccer.

4 _____
to ice-skate.

37 **Write.**

1 **A:** I like volleyball.   **B:** Me, _____!

2 **A:** I don't like milk.   **B:** Me _____.

38 **Read and circle.**

1 When we throw, we use our **feet** / **hands**.
2 When we jump, we use our **arms** / **legs**.
3 When we kick, we use our **feet** / **fingers**.
4 When we dance, we use our **nose** / **toes**.

I Can

☐ say what people like doing/to do.
☐ talk about how my body works.
☐ talk about playing safely.

In My House

50

1 Listen, look, and say.

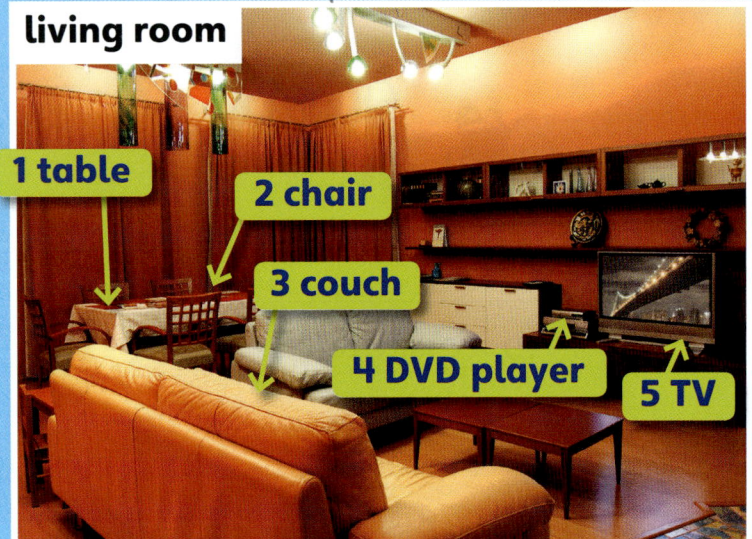

living room

1 table
2 chair
3 couch
4 DVD player
5 TV

bathroom

6 bathtub

kitchen

7 fridge
8 sink
9 oven

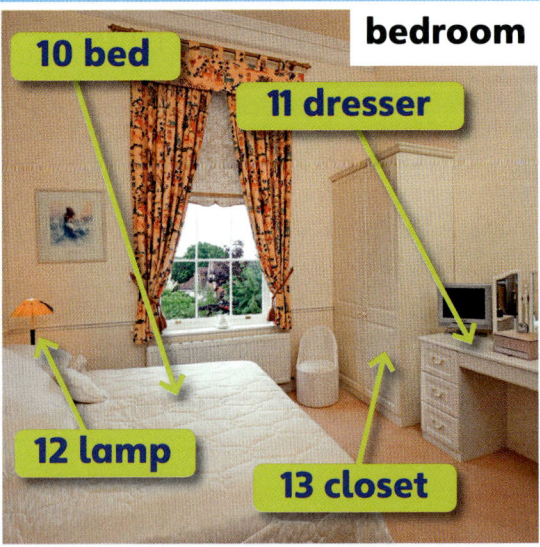

bedroom

10 bed
11 dresser
12 lamp
13 closet

51

2 Listen, find, and say.   **3** Play a game.

4 Listen and sing. Then look at 1 and find.

Where Are My Keys?

Where are my keys, Mom?
Your keys are on the chair.
The chair? Which chair?
There are chairs everywhere!

There's a chair in the living room
And one in the bedroom, too.
There are chairs in the dining room.
I don't know which chair. Do you?

Your keys are where you left them.
Put on your glasses and see.
They're on the chair behind you.
My keys are there! Silly me!

5 Listen and look at 1. Say yes or no.

6 Look at 1. Ask and answer.

Where's the bathtub?

It's in the bathroom.

THINK BIG What rooms in a house do we use for washing?
What rooms in a house do we use for eating?

56

 Listen and read. How many cousins does Jamie have?

1. Who are they, Jamie?

   They're my aunt and uncle. My aunt is my mom's sister.

2. These are my cousins. They're my aunt and uncle's children.

3. Where are your cousins now?

   They're in the kitchen. Look!

4. Where are they now?

   They're in my bedroom. They're jumping on my bed!

8 Look and write.

bedroom   living room   kitchen

1 Jamie's cousins are in the _____.

2 Now they're in Jamie's _____.

3 The TV is in the _____.

TH NK BIG My father's brother is my…
My father's sister is my…
My uncle's son is my…

9 Listen. Help Jamie and Jenny make sentences.

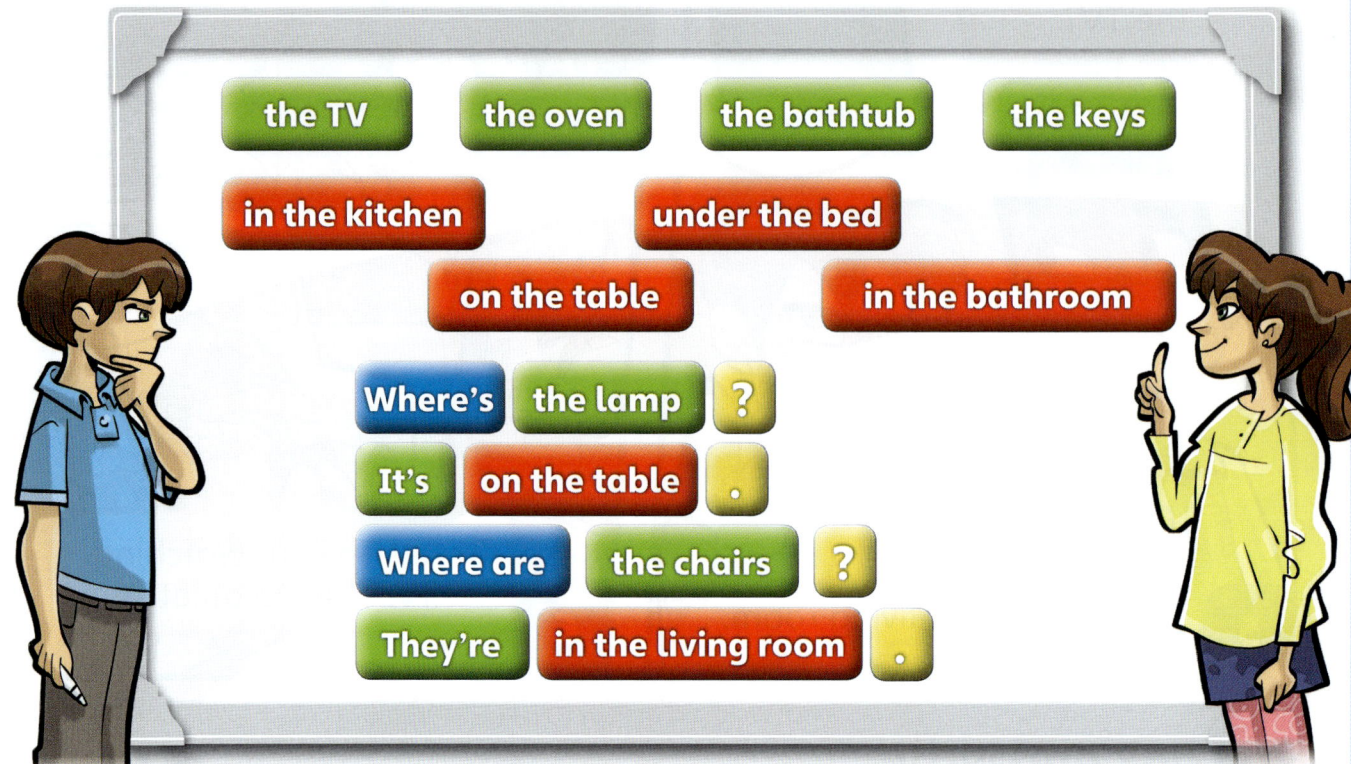

10 Look and write. Use **Where's** or **Where are**.

between   behind   in front of   next to

1 _____ the table?

It's _____ the TV and the couch.

2 _____ the lamps?

They're _____ the couch.

3 _____ the chair?

_____ the table.

4 _____ the TV?

_____ the table.

58

 11 **Listen and stick. Then ask and answer.**

Where are Ben's shoes?

Ben's shoes are in the kitchen.

12 **Write and draw. Where's your uncle's phone?**

My uncle's phone is

_____

_____ .

13 **Look at the pictures. What are they? Talk with a partner.**

bike   computer   lamp   TV

I think Picture b is a computer.

Really? I think it's a TV.

59

14 **Look, listen, and read. Then check your answers in 13.**

CONTENT WORDS

burn   museum   new   oil   old   screen   wheel

a

Emma White

At the Museum

1   Do you like to go to museums? I do! My favorite museum is the Science Museum. I love the old things there.

There are some very old lamps at the museum. They're nearly 2,000 years old. They need oil in them. The oil burns.

b

c

2   There's an old computer at the museum, too. You can put a new computer on a desk or in a backpack, but this computer needs a big room.

3   This old TV at the museum is very funny. It's big, but the screen is small. I don't want it in my living room!

d

4   My favorite thing at the museum is an old bike. One of its wheels is very big and one wheel is very small. When you ride it, you sit on the big wheel. It's great!

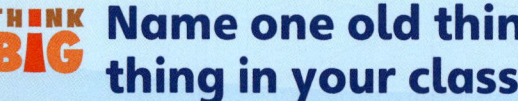

THINK BIG **Name one old thing and one new thing in your classroom and home.**

15 Look at 14. Circle **T** for true and **F** for false.

1 Emma likes museums.   T F

2 The lamps in the museum are old.   T F

3 You can put the old computer in a backpack.   T F

4 The old TV has a big screen.   T F

5 Emma wants the old TV in her living room.   T F

6 Emma likes the bike at the museum.   T F

16 Old or new? Play a game.

1  2  3  4

5  6  7  8

It's an old bathtub.

They're new boots.

Picture 4.

Picture 2.

PROJECT

17 Make a **New** and **Old** poster. Then present it to the class.

Old

Ye Olde Manuscript

New

This car is old. This jacket is new. I like this new car.

content connection (old and new things) Unit 3 **43**

Grammar

18 Listen and read. Then say.

Mom:	Come on, girls! Where are your coats? Jack's wearing his.
Carla:	We can't find ours.
Mom:	Yours is there, Carla, under the table.
Carla:	No, it isn't. That's Anna's coat. Hers is red. Mine is blue.
Mom:	Oh, dear! Look! The dogs think your coat is theirs!

19 Read. Then circle the words in **18**.

I have a bag.	The bag is **mine**.
You have a bag.	The bag is **yours**.
He has a bag.	The bag is **his**.
She has a bag.	The bag is **hers**.
We have a bag.	The bag is **ours**.
They have a bag.	The bag is **theirs**.

I'm wearing **my coat**. ✔
I'm wearing **my**. ✗

Look at the coats. **Mine** is red, and **yours** is blue. ✔
Mine coat is red, and **yours coat** is blue. ✗

20 Read and circle.

1 Eva has a hat. Is this hat **hers / her**?
2 David and Jim have a boat. Is that boat **their / theirs**?
3 You have a green pen. Is this green pen **yours / your**?
4 We have a lot of books. Are those books **our / ours**?

21 **Read and write.**

I have a big bedroom at home. I share it with my
sister. Her bed is pink, and 1_____ (I) is green.
My closet is brown, and 2_____ (she) is black.
Sometimes my cousins play in our bedroom. There are
some games under my bed. Some of the games are
3_____ (we), and some are 4_____ (they).
My favorite game is Cluedo. What's 5_____ (you)?

Jessie

22 **Read and match.**

1 That's my phone. → That phone is   yours.
2 These are his keys. → These keys are   mine.
3 This is your dog.   → This dog is   his.

23 **Look and write. Then compare and say.**

What's your favorite…?	color	toy	sport
me			
	green	puppet	gymnastics
	red	dinosaur	volleyball
	blue	train	ice-skating

Her favorite color is green.   Mine is pink!

Household Objects

1   In Sudan, some people keep their food cold in clay pots. They put one pot in another, with wet sand between them. A fridge needs electricity, but these pots don't. They can keep food cold anywhere.

2   Some people in Mali cook with a solar oven. A solar oven doesn't need fuel. It uses the sun. When this oven is in the sun, it's very hot, and it cooks the food quickly. This woman is cooking yam.

24   Look at the pictures. Then match.

It's a different bed.	It's a different oven.
It's a different fridge.	They're different chairs.

62
25   Listen and read. Then match and write 1–4.

It can go in a closet.   ☐   They're Japanese.   ☐

It keeps food cold.   ☐   It works quickly.   ☐

26   Look at 25. Read and circle.

1   The clay pots **need / don't need** electricity.

2   The sand between the pots is **dry / wet**.

3   The solar oven needs **fuel / sun**.

4   The Japanese chairs don't have **arms / legs**.

5   People with hammocks in Sarawak **use / don't use** beds.

4   Some people in Sarawak, Indonesia, sleep in hammocks. They don't use beds. The hammocks are clean and comfortable. When you don't need them, you can put them in a closet.

3   Do you like these chairs? This is a restaurant in Japan. The chairs don't have legs, but they're comfortable, and Japanese people like them.

27 🗨 **Find the words. Then write.**

At home, we keep food cold in a ¹_____.
When we cook food, we use an ²_____.
When we eat dinner, we sit on ³_____s.
We sleep in ⁴_____s.

THINK BIG **Do you want the things in the pictures in your home? Why/Why not?**

28 **Listen and write. Then say.**

| sink toy box |
| washing machine |

1 I put my toys in the _____.

2 I put my dirty dishes in the _____.

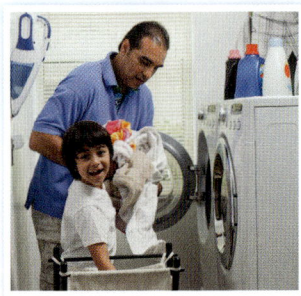

3 I put my dirty clothes in the

_____.

29 **How do you keep your home neat? Act it out. Then guess.**

You put your clothes in the closet.

THINK BIG Is it good to be neat at home? Why?
Is it good to be neat in class? Why?

66
 30 **Listen, look, and repeat.**

1 OO   **2** OO

67
 31 **Listen and find. Then say.**

m**oo**n

b**oo**k

z**oo**

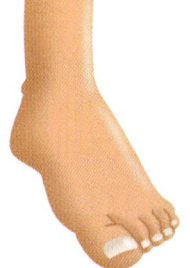

f**oo**t

68
 32 **Listen and blend the sounds.**

1 r-oo-m   room   **2** l-oo-k   look

3 f-oo-d   food   **4** c-oo-k   cook

5 c-oo-l   cool   **6** g-oo-d   good

69
 33 **Underline oo and oo. Then listen and chant.**

Look in my cookbook.
The food is good!
The food is cool!

34 **Look and choose a room. Draw a line.**

keys

phone

soccer ball

glasses

roller skates

hat

35 **Look at 34. Ask and answer.**

Where are the keys?

They're on the table in front of the bed.

36 **Look and write. Use old or new.**

bathtubs
chairs
dresser
fridge
lamp
oven

1 This _____ is _____.

2 This _____ is _____.

3 This is a _____ _____.

 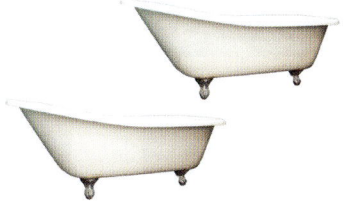 

4 This is a _____ _____.

5 These _____ are _____.

6 These are _____ _____.

37 **Read and write.**

brother's   his   mine   yours

James: Kate, are these glasses on the table _____?

Kate: No, they're my _____ glasses. I'm wearing _____!

James: Oh, yes! Is this your brother's book?

Kate: Yes, that's _____.

I Can

☐ **say where things are.**

☐ **talk about possessions.**

☐ **talk about new and old objects.**

Do I Know It?

1 ▶ Think about it. Look and circle. Practice.

😊 I know this.   😕 I don't know this.

1		😊 😕	p. 4
2		😊 😕	p. 20
3		😊 😕	p. 36
4		😊 😕	p. 36

5	What's he doing? He's reading a book.	😊 😕	p. 8
6	How many computers are there? There's one computer./There are three computers.	😊 😕	p. 9
7	Don't stand on the table. Be careful!	😊 😕	p. 12
8	What do they like doing? They like flying kites.	😊 😕	p. 24
9	I like volleyball. I don't like tennis.	😊 😕	p. 28
10	She loves to swim. Me, too!	😊 😕	p. 28
11	Where's the table? It's in the kitchen.	😊 😕	p. 40
12	Is this yours? Yes, it's mine.	😊 😕	p. 44

71

2 **Get ready.**

A Look, listen, and write.

between   on   under

Miss Davis: What's your favorite game on the playground?
Beth: Mine is soccer.
Adam: I like playing ¹_____ the swings.
Katy: And I like skating!
Miss Davis: OK. Where's the soccer ball?
Beth: It's ²_____ the chair.
Miss Davis: And where are Katy's skates?
Adam: They're ³_____ the two chairs.
Miss Davis: OK, everybody. Take your things, and go outside. And be quick!

B Look at **A** and point. Ask and answer with a partner.

What's she doing?   She's coloring a picture.

C Look at **A**. Point and say how many. Use **There's** or **There are**.

chairs   soccer ball   teacher

1
2
3
4
5
6
7
8
9

3 **Get set.**

 Cut out the cards on page 181.
Now you're ready to **Go!**

72

 4 **Go!**

A Look at the cards and write. Listen and check.

are   coloring   on   reading   they're   under

1 In pictures 1 and 2, they're _____ a picture.

2 In pictures 3 and 4, _____ playing soccer.

3 In pictures 1 and 3, they're _____ a book.

4 In pictures 2 and 4, there's a basketball _____ the table.

5 In pictures 1, 2, 3, and 4, there _____ keys _____ the table.

B Point to a card. Ask and answer with a partner.

What do they like doing?

They like playing soccer.

Where are the keys?

They're on the table.

5 Write or draw.

All About Me

What do you like doing in your classroom?	Where do you like reading?
What do you like doing on the playground?	What don't you like?

Do I Know It Now?

6 Think about it.

A Go to page **52**. Look and circle again.

B Check (✔).

☐ I can start the next unit.

☐ I can ask my teacher for help and then start the next unit.

☐ I can practice and then start the next unit.

7 Rate this Checkpoint. Color the stars.

 easy  hard    fun  not fun

Units 1–3 Exam Preparation

– Part A –

 Listen and draw lines. There is one example.

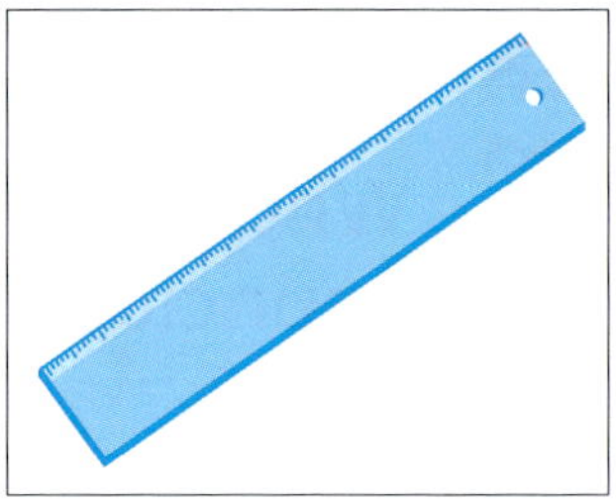

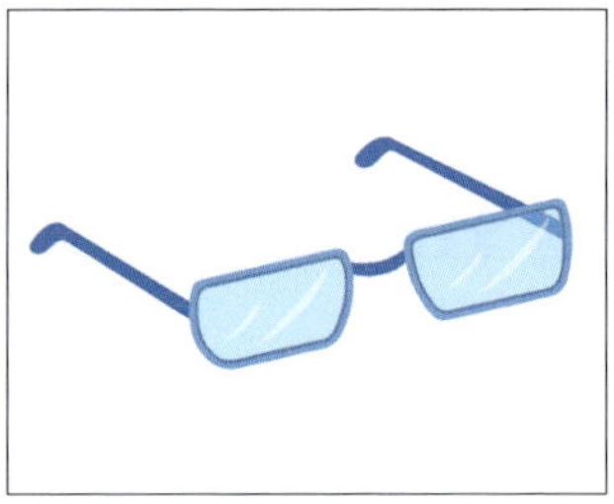

Look and read. Write *yes* or *no*.

Examples

A boy is climbing a tree. _____ *yes*

There's a blue kite in the tree. _____ *no*

Questions

1 There's a girl on a bike. _____

2 Two girls are playing soccer. _____

3 A man is listening to music. _____

4 A woman is running behind a cat. _____

5 There are two trees. _____

unit 4

In My Town

1 Listen, look, and say.

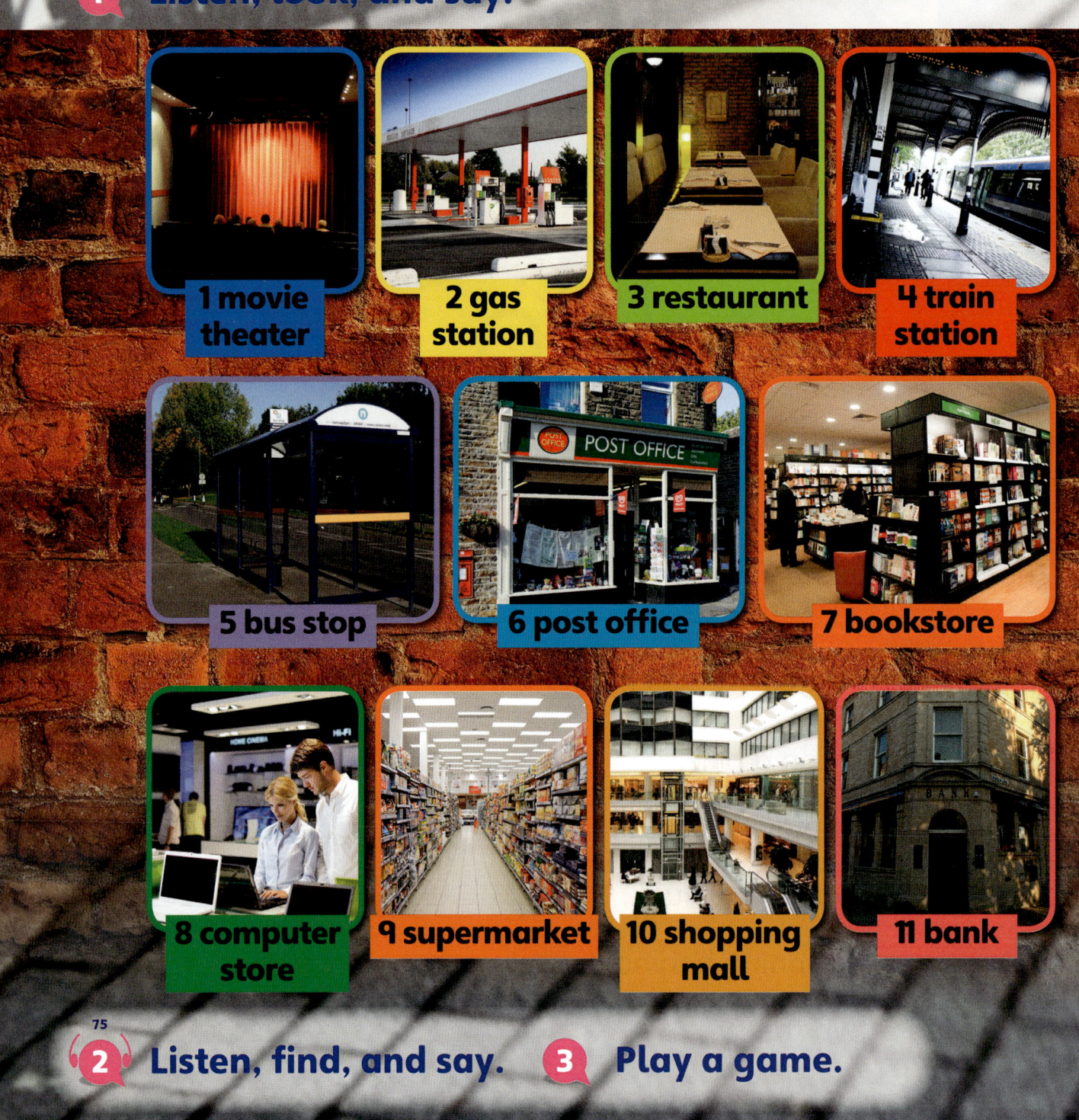

1 movie theater

2 gas station

3 restaurant

4 train station

5 bus stop

6 post office

7 bookstore

8 computer store

9 supermarket

10 shopping mall

11 bank

2 Listen, find, and say.   **3 Play a game.**

4 **Listen and sing. Then look at 1 and find.**

Maps Are Great!

Where's the bookstore?
I want to buy a book.
Here, I have a map.
Come on. Let's take a look!

The bookstore is on River Street.
It isn't far from us.
Do you want to walk there?
No, thanks! Let's take the bus!

I want to send a letter, too.
Is there a post office?
Do you know?
I'm looking at the map.
Yes, there is.
It's near the bookstore.
Come on. Let's go.

Maps are really great.
I use them every day.
In town or out of town,
They help me find my way!

78

5 **Listen and number.**

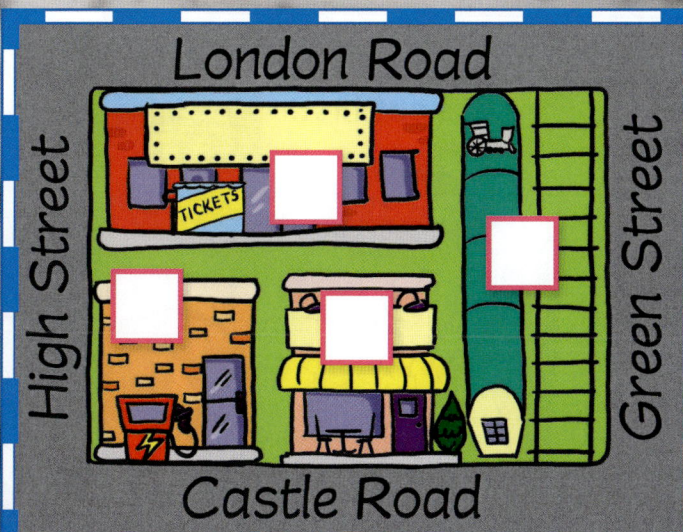

6 **Look at 5. Ask and answer.**

Where's the restaurant?

It's on Castle Road. It's next to the gas station.

THINK BIG **What can you see at a bus stop?**
What can you eat in a restaurant?

80

7 Listen and read. Where are Jenny and her dad?

Is There a Bookstore?

Panel 1

Do you want to come to the shopping mall, Jenny?

Yes, OK.

Panel 2

I want to buy a book. Is there a bookstore?

Yes, there is. Look!

Panel 3

I want to buy a computer game. Is there a computer store?

Yes, there is. It's here.

Panel 4

I'm hungry. Let's eat first.

OK. There are restaurants over there!

8 Look and read. Write.

1 Jenny's dad wants to buy a book at the _____.

2 Jenny wants to buy a _____ _____ at the computer store.

3 Jenny and her dad want to eat lunch at a _____.

4 Jenny wants pizza and _____.

5 Dad doesn't have his _____.

THINK BIG **Do you like shopping?**
Where do you go shopping?
What's your favorite store?
What do you like buying?

9 Listen. Help Jamie and Jenny make sentences.

81

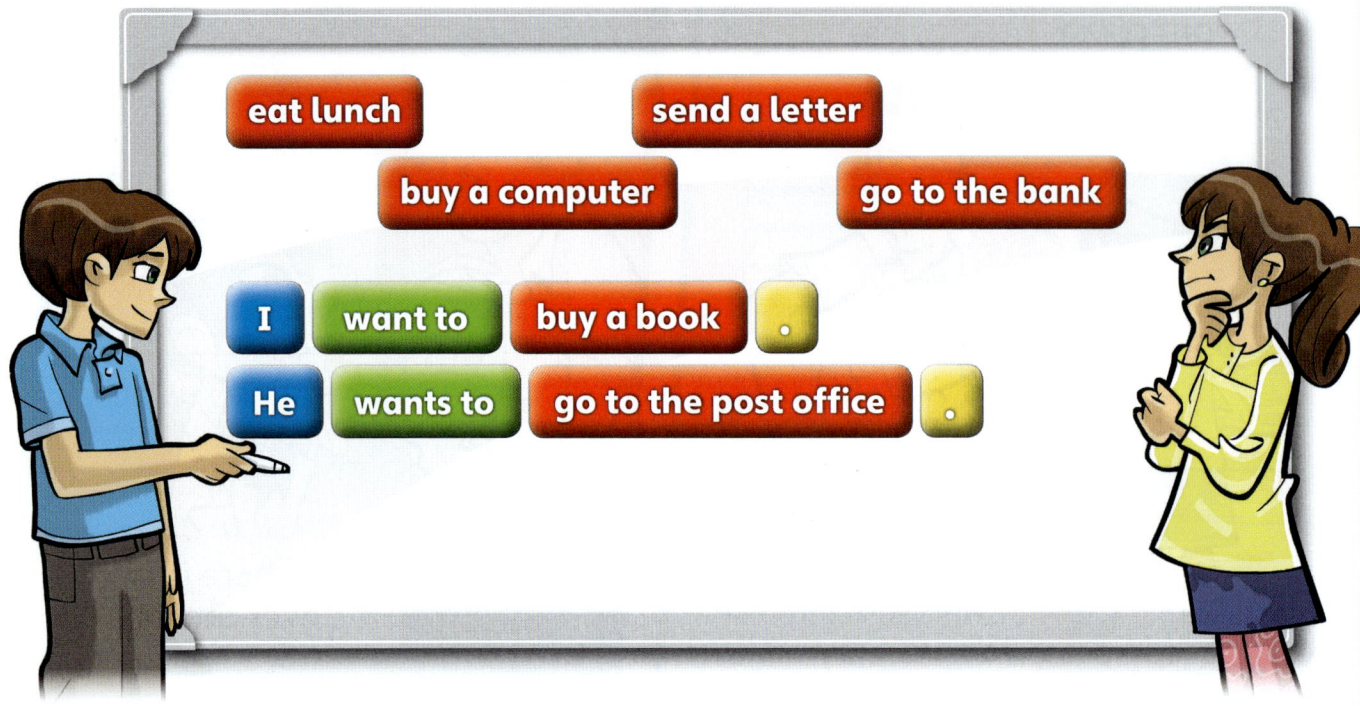

eat lunch   send a letter

buy a computer   go to the bank

I   want to   buy a book   .

He   wants to   go to the post office   .

10 Write want to or wants to.

1 Mom _____ buy bananas.

2 I _____ buy a new jacket.

3 My brother and I _____ eat sandwiches.

4 Paula and Richard _____ watch a movie.

5 We _____ go to the bus stop.

6 My cousin _____ buy a soccer ball.

7 They _____ go to the bank.

8 I _____ send a letter.

11 **Listen and stick. Then say.**

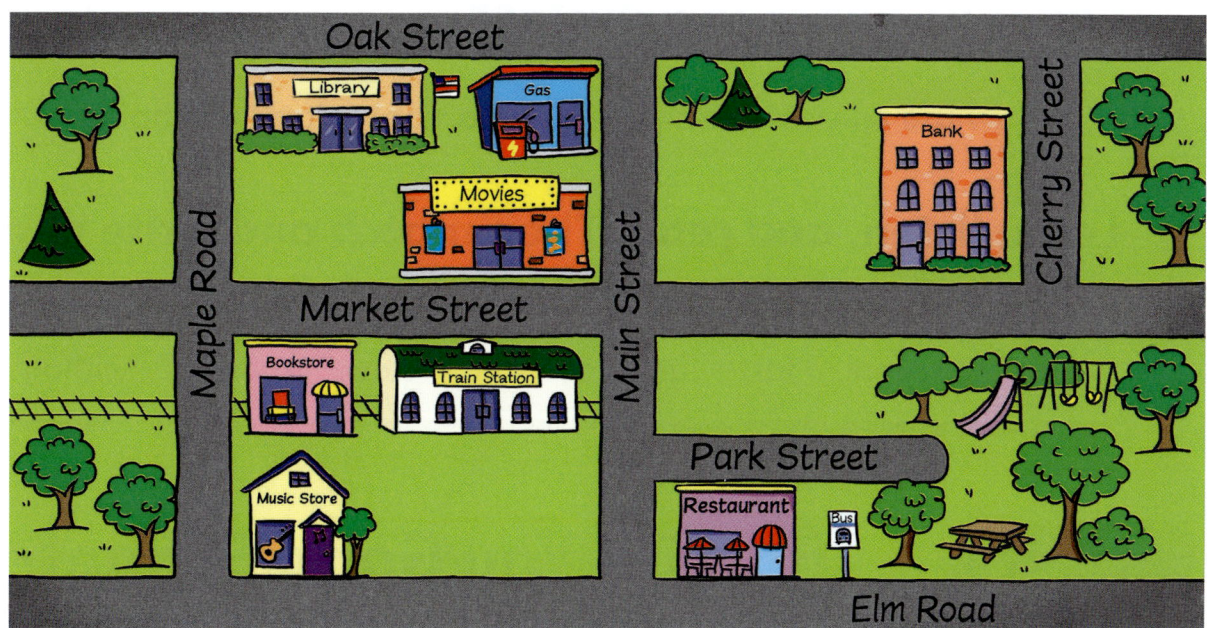

12 **Look at 11. Ask and answer.**

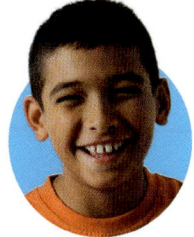

Is there a bank near here?

Yes, there is. It's on Cherry Street.

Is there a post office on Elm Road?

No, there isn't. It's on Park Street next to the park.

13 **Write and draw. Where's the shopping mall?**

The shopping mall is

_____

_____

_____ .

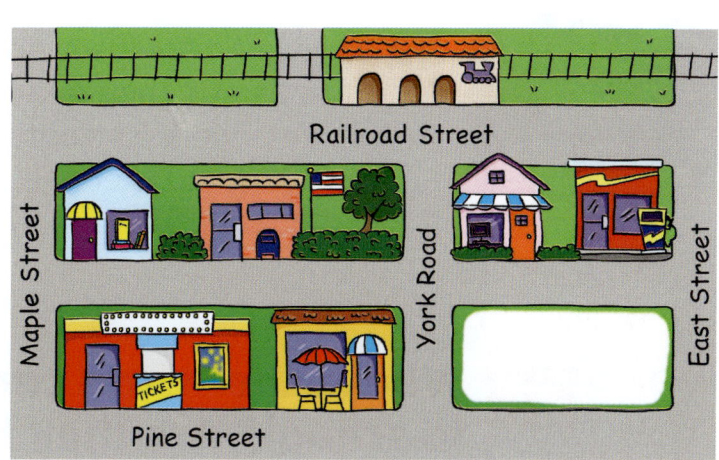

14 Look at pictures **a–d** in **15**. Which transportation do you use? Talk with a partner.

> I use bikes and trains.

> Me, too! I don't use boats.

15 Look, listen, and read. Then match and write **a–d**.

CONTENT WORDS

boat   canal   fast   ground   safe   slow   subway   without

a

b

c

d

How Do You Go to School?

1 I live in Bangkok, and I go to school by boat. There are a lot of canals here, and there are a lot of boats on the canals.
Sunan

2 Here in Mexico City, there are a lot of cars on the streets. Going by car is slow. I always go to school by bus. It's fast, and the bus stop is near my school.
Carmen

3 I go to school by subway train. It goes under the ground. There are a lot of subway trains here in New York, and there are 468 stations! One of the stations is very close to our apartment.
Sophia

4 I live in Amsterdam, and I go to school by bike. My friends ride their bikes, too. There are a lot of "bike streets" here – streets without cars. They're safe, and it's good exercise.
Lars

THINK BIG What other ways can you use to go to school? Are they fast or slow?

16 **Look at 15. Read and write the names.**

1 _____ exercises when he goes to school.

2 _____ lives near a station.

3 _____ goes to a school with a bus stop near it.

4 _____ lives in a place with a lot of canals.

5 _____ lives in a place with safe streets for bikes.

6 _____ goes under the ground when she goes to school.

17 **Do a class survey. Ask and answer.**

	bus	train	boat	bike	other
Sam	✔				

Sam, how do you go to school?

I go to school by bus.

PROJECT

18 **Make a Go to School bar chart. Then present it to the class.**

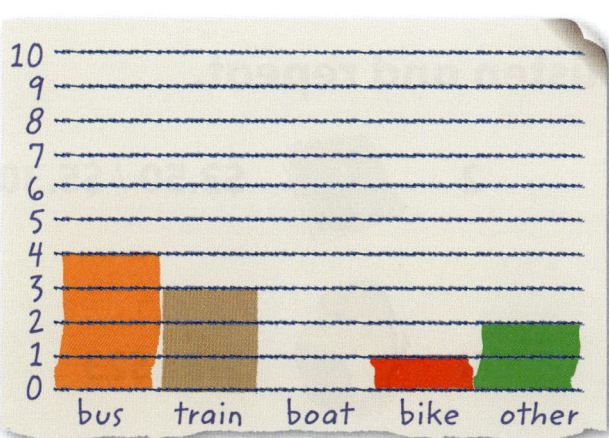

In my class, four children go to school by bus.

19 85 **Listen and read. Then say.**

Sales clerk:	Hello. Can I help you?
Mary:	Yes, please. How much is this pencil case?
Sales clerk:	It's six dollars.
Mary:	And how much are those notebooks?
Sales clerk:	They're four dollars and fifty cents.
Mary:	Can I buy a green notebook, please?

20 **Read. Then circle How much, dollars, and cents in 19.**

How much	is	it? this pencil case? that train?
	are	they? these pens? those notebooks?

It's	twelve **dollars**.
	twenty-five **cents**.
They're	four **dollars** and fifty **cents**.

A hundred cents (100¢) = one dollar ($1).

21 86 **Listen and circle. Then listen and repeat.**

1  29¢ / 99¢

2  $3.50 / $5.30

3 ... $3.90 / $9.90

4 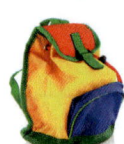 $13 / $23

22 Look and write.

1  $8

2  $19.50

3  $3

4 $9.99

1 How much is the ball?
It's _____ dollars.

2 How much are the shoes?
They're _____ dollars and _____ cents.

3 _____ _____ is the hat?
It's _____ _____.

4 _____ _____ is the game?
_____ _____ _____ and
_____-_____ _____.

23 Read and number in order.

☐ **A:** OK.

☐ **B:** Yes, please. How much are these cookies?

☐ **A:** They're two dollars and thirty-five cents.

☐ **A:** Hi. Can I help you?

☐ **B:** Can I buy them, please?

24 Look at 22 and 23. Role-play.

Hello. Can I help you?

Yes, please. How much are...?

Taxi!

There are taxis in every city in the world, but they aren't all the same. Here are some of our favorites.

1

In London, most of the taxis are big and black. They have a famous design. They're modern, but they look like cars from a long time ago. They're comfortable and fun to ride in. ☐

a

2

In Berlin, taxis are comfortable, but they aren't very colorful. They're very light brown, with a black and yellow taxi sign on top. Most of them look the same. ☐

b

25 **Look at the pictures. What kind of car do they show?**

88
26 **Listen and read. Then match and write a–d.**

27 **Look at 26. Circle T for true or F for false.**

1 Havana has some old taxis. T F

2 The big black taxis in London aren't very old. T F

3 The taxis in Berlin are all different colors. T F

4 All the taxis in New Delhi have three wheels. T F

THINK BIG **Why do people take taxis? Which taxi in the pictures do you like? Why?**

3 **In New Delhi**, a lot of taxis have only three wheels! They're green and yellow, and they have a special name: tuk tuk. They aren't very fast, but they're cheap and easy to find. ☐

c

4 **In Havana**, there are a lot of colorful taxis. Some of them are old, but these black and yellow taxis are new and modern. They have three wheels, and they're really fun. ☐

d

28 **Complete for a city you know. Then write.**

Name of city _____

Taxis   old ☐   new ☐   big ☐   small ☐

     color(s) _____

Buses   old ☐   new ☐   big ☐   small ☐

     color(s) _____

In New York, there are a lot of taxis. They're big and new. Most of them are yellow. There are a lot of buses, too. Most of them are blue and white, but school buses are yellow.

In..., there are a lot of...
They're...
Most of them are...

90
29  **Listen and write. Then say.**

cross   look   wait

1 First, I always _____ at the pedestrian crossing.

2 Second, I _____ for the green man.

3 Last, I _____ left, then right, then left again before I cross the street.

30 **Look and number. Then ask and answer.**

a

b

c

How do you cross the street safely?

First, I always cross at the pedestrian crossing.

 **THINK BIG** **What animal does a pedestrian crossing look like? Does a pedestrian crossing always have lights? Find out.**

91

 Listen, look, and repeat.

1 ai   **2** oa

92

 Listen and find. Then say.

train

rain

coat

boat

93

 **Listen and blend the sounds.**

1 n-ai-l   nail   **2** oa-k   oak

3 t-ai-l   tail   **4** s-oa-p   soap

5 w-ai-t   wait   **6** r-oa-d   road

94

 Underline ai and oa. Then listen and chant.

Wear a coat
To sail the boat!
Drive the train
In the rain!

35 **Work in two groups. Make sentence cards.**

Group A:
Write sentences starting with *I want to.* Write a different activity for each student in the group.

Group B:
Write sentences starting with *There's a.* Write a different place for each student in the group.

36 **Groups A and B: Take turns reading your cards. Find your match.**

I want to buy a book.

There's a bookstore near here.

Yes, a match!

37 **Read and match.**

1 I want to buy a book.
2 Tim wants to see a movie.
3 Mom and Dad want to put gas in the car.
4 Ben wants to send a letter.

a There's a movie theater near the bus stop.
b There's a post office on Main Street.
c There's a bookstore on Maple Road.
d There's a gas station next to the bank.

38 **Look and write. Use by.**

1 Many children go to school
_____.

2 My sister comes home
_____.

3 My mom goes to the bank
_____.

39 **Read and circle.**

Maria: Mom, **I want** / **wants** to buy a ruler.
Mom: **How many** / **How much** is it?
Maria: It's two **dollar ten cents** / **dollars and ten cents**.
Mom: OK.

I Can

☐ say what I want and talk about money.
☐ describe where places are in town.
☐ talk about different kinds of transportation.

My Dream Job

97

1 Listen, look, and say.

1 actor   **2 artist**   **3 dancer**   **4 doctor**

5 writer   **6 pilot**   **7 singer**

8 athlete   **9 teacher**   **10 chef**   **11 vet**

98

2 Listen, find, and say.   **3** Play a game.

4 **Listen and chant. Then look at 1 and find.**

Hey, What Do You Want to Be?

Hey, what do you want to be?
You have to choose just one.
There are so many different jobs.
I want one that is fun!

I want to be a dancer
And an athlete, too.
Or maybe a teacher.
What about you?

I want to be an actor,
And I want to be a vet.
I want to be a pilot, too.
Then I can fly a jet!

Chorus

101

5 **Listen and write.**

1 I want to be a _____.

2 I want to be a _____.

3 I want to be a _____.

6 **Look at 1. Ask and answer.**

What do you want to be?

I want to be a chef.

TH_NK BIG **What jobs do people do at school?**
What jobs do people do in town?

7 Listen and read. What does Jamie like doing?

103

Dream Jobs!

1

What do you want to be, Jenny?

I want to be a singer. I like singing.

2

What do you want to be, Dan?

I want to be a writer. I like writing stories.

3

What's your dream job, Maria?

I want to be a dancer. I like dancing.

4

Jamie, your sister wants to be a singer. What do you want to be?

I want to be a chef.

8 Look at the story. Write.

1 Jenny wants to be a _____.
2 Dan wants to be a _____.
3 Maria wants to be a _____.
4 Jamie wants to be a _____.

THINK BIG What's your favorite job in the story? Why?
What do you want to be? Why?

9 **Listen. Help Jamie and Jenny make sentences.**

| an artist | a pilot |
| an athlete | a chef |

What do you	want to be	?
I want to be	an actor	.
What does he	want to be	?
He wants to be	a doctor	.

10 **Look and write. Then draw and write.**

1 What does she want to be?

_____

2 What does he want to be?

_____

3 What does Sally want to be?

_____

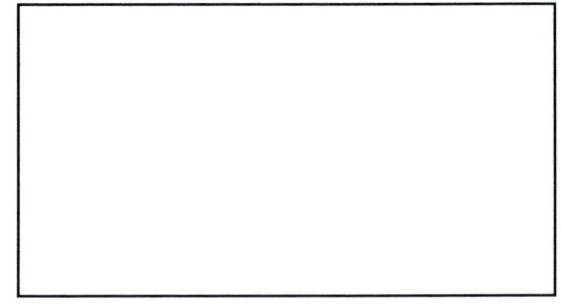

4 What do you want to be?

_____

11 Listen and stick. Then say.
105

1

2

3

4

12 Look at 11. Ask and answer.

What does he want to be?

He wants to be a singer.

13 Write. Use do or does.
1 What _____ he want to be?

2 What _____ they want to be?

3 What _____ your cousins want to be?

4 What _____ your brother/sister want to be?

14 Look at the pictures. What are the jobs? How do they help us?

106
15 Look, listen, and read. Then circle.

> **CONTENT WORDS**
> carpenter   entertain   farmer   hairdresser
> nurse   produce   provide   take care of   waiter

Goods and Services

Businesses want to make money. There are two ways to do this. They can produce goods, or they can provide services.

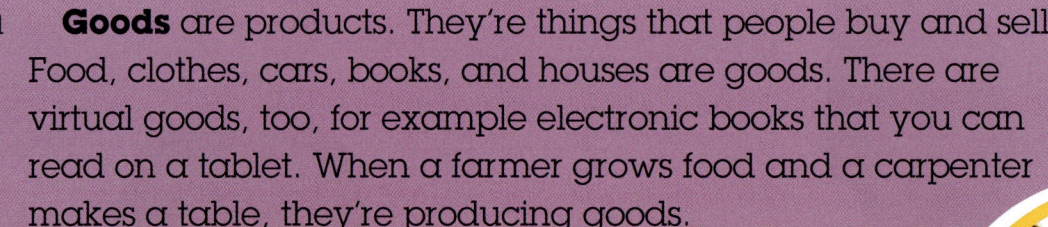

1 **Goods** are products. They're things that people buy and sell. Food, clothes, cars, books, and houses are goods. There are virtual goods, too, for example electronic books that you can read on a tablet. When a farmer grows food and a carpenter makes a table, they're producing goods.

2 **Services** are activities that people do for others. When a hairdresser cuts your hair and a nurse takes care of you, they're providing a service. Actors and singers provide a service, too: they entertain you.

3 Some businesses provide goods and services together. For example, a restaurant sells goods: the food and drink. But it provides services, too: the waiters take the food to the table, and other people wash the dishes after the meal.

grow food:
goods / services
cutting hair:
goods / services
a restaurant:
goods / goods and services

> **THINK BIG** Do people in these jobs produce goods, provide services, or both?
> pilot   artist   baker

16 **Look at 15. Circle T for true and F for false.**

1 Businesses make money with goods and services.　　**T**　**F**

2 People buy and sell goods.　　**T**　**F**

3 Services are products.　　**T**　**F**

4 Actors produce goods.　　**T**　**F**

5 Waiters wash the dishes in a restaurant.　　**T**　**F**

17 **Look and match. Then ask and answer.**

actors	take	sick people
waiters	grow	food to tables
hairdressers	take care of	food
farmers	cut	people
nurses	entertain	hair

What do actors do?

They entertain people.

PROJECT

18 **Make a Goods and Services poster. Then present it to the class.**

Goods　Services

milk　a table　flying a plane

Here are some goods: milk, a table...

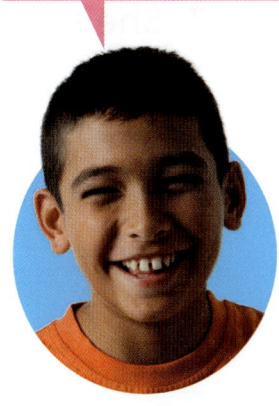

108

19 Listen and read. Then say.

Harry:	Hi, Jasmine. Do you want to go to the park?
Jasmine:	Sorry, I can't. I'm with my dad at the mechanic's because our car isn't working.
Harry:	Oh, well. Maybe I can go with Gemma or Luke.
Jasmine:	No, Luke is at the hairdresser's because he wants a new hairstyle. And Gemma is at the vet's because her dog looks sick.
Harry:	Oh, dear! Maybe we can go tomorrow…

20 Read. Then circle because in 19.

> Tim wants to be a doctor. He loves science.
> → Tim wants to be a doctor **because** he loves science.
>
> Gemma is at the vet's. Her cat looks sick.
> → Gemma is at the vet's **because** her cat looks sick.

> The weather **looks nice**. Let's have a picnic.
> You **look tired**. Are you OK?

21 Read and match.

1 She's at the doctor's
2 She's at school
3 She's at the bank
4 She's at a restaurant
5 She's at the computer store

a because she's a chef.
b because her computer isn't working.
c because she needs money.
d because she's a teacher.
e because she feels sick.

22 **Read and circle.**

1 My uncle goes to a restaurant every day because he's **a doctor / a waiter**.

2 My sister wants to be a nurse because she loves to **help people / grow food**.

3 David wants to be **a carpenter / a hairdresser** because he loves to make things.

4 I think that man is **an actor / a carpenter** because he looks funny.

5 I think that woman is a nurse because **she looks kind / she looks sick**.

23 **Look and write. Use because.**

at the beach   at the hairdresser's
at the supermarket   in the kitchen

1 She's _____ she wants a new hairstyle.

2 They're _____ they need food.

3 He's _____ he wants to be a chef.

4 She's _____ she loves the ocean.

24 **Draw and write.**

I'm _____

_____

(where?) because

_____

_____

(why?).

When I Grow Up

What do you want to be when you're older? These kids know.

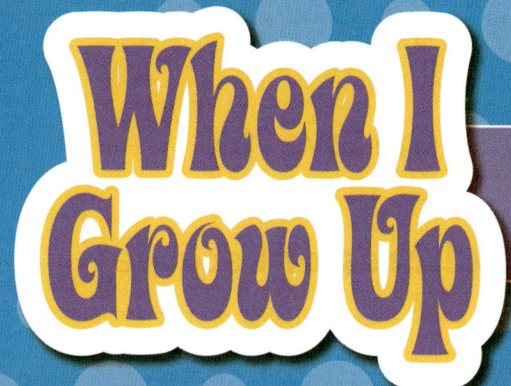

1   I'm José Antonio. My home is near the ocean in Costa Rica. I love to swim and look at the colorful fish here. My mom is a photographer. I sometimes use her underwater camera. It takes great pictures. When I grow up, I want to be a scuba diver and work underwater.

25 **Look at the pictures. Find the jobs.**

park ranger   rodeo rider   scuba diver

26 **Listen and read. What do they like?**

109

27 **Look at 26. Read and circle.**

  1 José Antonio likes to **swim** / **catch fish**.

  2 Katie's family has a lot of **children** / **cows**.

  3 **Juma** / **Juma's** father is a park ranger.

THINK BIG **Which jobs help animals in your city? What do you want to be? Why?**

2   My name is Katie. I'm from Oklahoma, in the United States. My family lives on a ranch, and we have a lot of cows and horses. I love our ranch. When I finish school, I want to be a vet and help sick animals. In my free time, I want to ride in the rodeo!

3   My name is Juma. I live with my family in Botswana, in Africa. I love the beautiful animals here. Some of them are in danger. This is a picture of my father. One day, I want to be a park ranger like him and help protect wild animals.

28 Ask three friends. Then write.

What do you want to be?

What do farmers do?

I want to be a farmer.

They grow food and work with animals.

Name	What/want to be?	What/do?

 **Listen and write. Then say.**

art   math   music   science

1 I like _____.
I want to be a teacher.

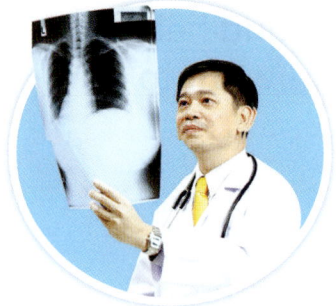

2 I like _____.
I want to be a doctor.

3 I like _____.
I want to be a pilot.

4 I like _____.
I want to be an artist.

30 **Tell a partner what you want to be. Then act it out.**

I like music. I want to be a singer.

I like music, too. I want to be a dancer.

THINK BIG **You like _____. What other jobs can you do?**

a art   **b** music   **c** math   **d** science

31 **Listen, look, and repeat.**

1 ar **2** er **3** or

32 **Listen and find. Then say.**

arm

car

teacher

cor**n**

33 **Listen and blend the sounds.**

1 c-ar-t cart **2** s-i-ng-er singer

3 f-or for **4** ar-t art

5 b-or-n born **6** l-e-tt-er letter

34 **Underline ar, er, and or. Then listen and chant.**

I want to be a singer
Or an artist painting art.
I want to be a teacher
Or a farmer with a cart!

35 **Work in small groups. Ask, "What do you want to be?" Write names and jobs.**

Name	Wants to Be
Michael	a pilot

36 **Count how many students in 35 want each job. Write a list.**

Job	How Many
Doctor	3

37 **Look at this bar chart. Make a bar chart for your group and talk about it.**

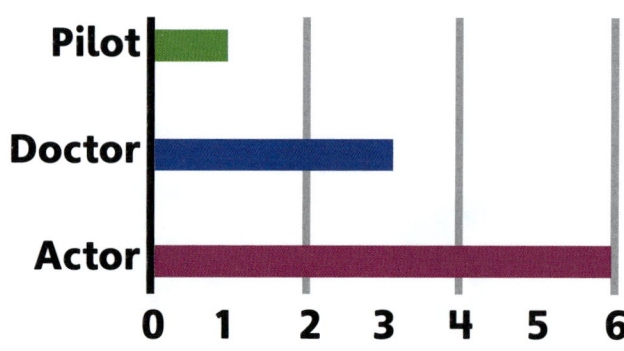

One student wants to be a pilot. Three students want to be doctors.

38 **Look and write.** | dancer   singer   teacher   writer

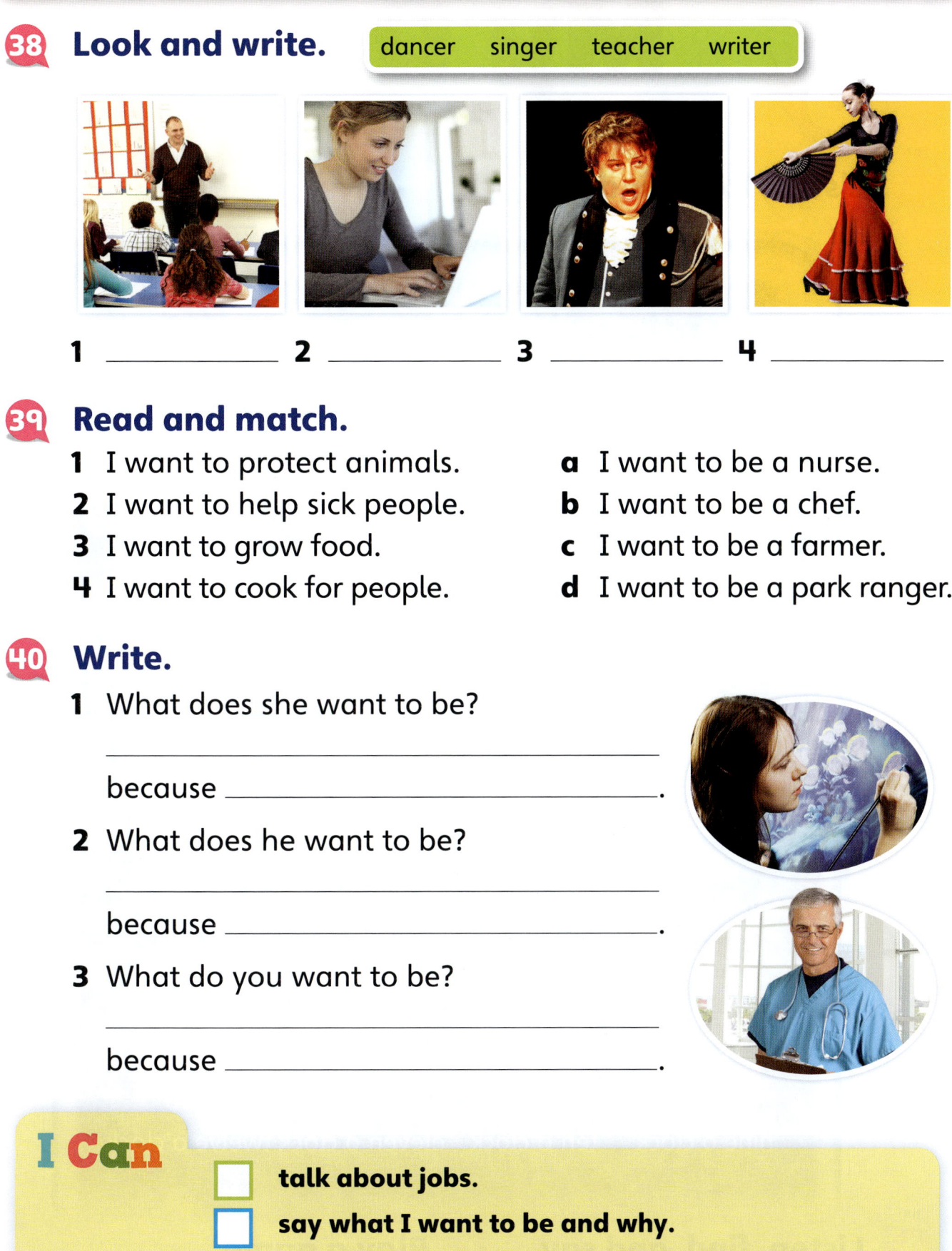

1 _____ 2 _____ 3 _____ 4 _____

39 **Read and match.**

1 I want to protect animals.
2 I want to help sick people.
3 I want to grow food.
4 I want to cook for people.

a I want to be a nurse.
b I want to be a chef.
c I want to be a farmer.
d I want to be a park ranger.

40 **Write.**

1 What does she want to be?

_____

because _____.

2 What does he want to be?

_____

because _____.

3 What do you want to be?

_____

because _____.

I Can

☐ **talk about jobs.**
☐ **say what I want to be and why.**
☐ **talk about studying hard and setting goals.**

My Day

 1 **Listen, look, and say.**

1:00	**2:00**	**3:00**	**4:00**
one o'clock	two o'clock	three o'clock	four o'clock
5:00	**6:00**	**7:00**	**8:00**
five o'clock	six o'clock	seven o'clock	eight o'clock
9:00	**10:00**	**11:00**	**12:00**
nine o'clock	ten o'clock	eleven o'clock	twelve o'clock

 2 **Listen, find, and say.**   **3** **Play a game.**

4 Listen and sing. Then look at 1 and find.

What Time Is It?

Tick, tock. It's seven o'clock.
Time to get up and get dressed.
I want to stay in bed,
But it's time to brush my teeth!

Tick, tock. It's eight o'clock.
At nine o'clock, I start school.
I eat my breakfast and get my books.
I love school, it's cool!

Tick, tock. It's three o'clock.
There's no more school today.
I do my homework, and I go out.
And there's my friend to play.

Now it's evening, and it's eight o'clock,
And it's time to go to bed.
I watch TV and read my book.
Time to sleep now, good night!

122

5 Look at 4. Listen and say yes or no.

6 Look at 1. Ask and answer.

What time is it?

It's one o'clock.

THINK BIG What time is it now?
What time is it at midday?
What time is it at midnight?

124

7 Listen and read. When does Max get up?

8 Look at the story. Number in order.

- ☐ Max comes home.
- ☐ Max gets up.
- ☐ Max eats.
- ☐ Max sleeps again.
- ☐ Max goes out.

THINK BIG What time do you go to bed?
What time do you get up?
How many hours do you sleep? Is that
good or bad?

125

9 Listen. Help Jamie and Jenny make sentences.

| go out | start school | watch TV | finish school |

| at 9:00 | at 7:00 | at 3:00 | at 12:00 |

When | does he get up | ?

He gets up | at 6:00 | .

When | do you go to bed | ?

I go to bed | at 8:00 | .

10 Look and write **do** or **does**. Then answer the questions.

1 When _____ she eat lunch?

She _____

_____ .

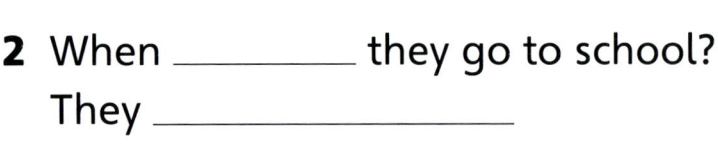

2 When _____ they go to school?

They _____

_____ .

3 When _____ he brush his teeth?

He _____

_____ .

11 Listen and stick. Then say.

1

2

3

4

12 Look at 11. Ask and answer.

When does she go to bed?

She goes to bed at ten o'clock.

13 Look and write. Use start and finish.

1 When does the movie start? It starts at

_____.

2 When does the movie end? It ends at

_____.

3 When _____ school _____?

_____
_____

4 _____ _____?

_____
_____

14 Look at the pictures. What do all the things do?

128

15 Look, listen, and read. Then match and write **a–d**.

> **CONTENT WORDS**
> burn   candle   cup   fall   height   hourglass   sand   shadow   sundial

a

Telling the Time

b

What time is it? How do you know? Today we look at clocks, watches, and cell phones, but here are some other ways to tell the time. Some are very old.

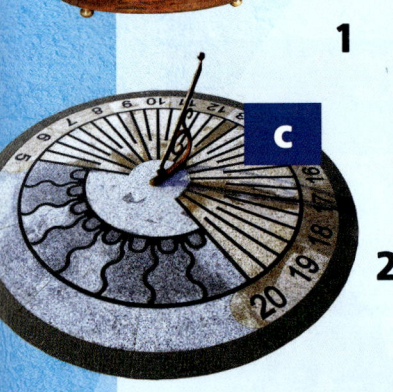

c

1 A sundial uses the sun to tell the time. The sun makes a shadow on the sundial, and the shadow tells the time. It's a great invention, but it isn't useful at night or when it's cloudy! ☐

d

2 A candle clock can work in the day or at night. When the candle burns, it gets shorter. The height of the candle tells you the time. ☐

3 An hourglass uses sand to tell the time. Sand falls from the top to the bottom. Some people use small hourglasses today when they're cooking eggs. ☐

4 A water clock uses water to tell the time. It works like an hourglass. It has two cups. The water falls from one cup to the other. ☐

THINK BIG Look, think, and draw.

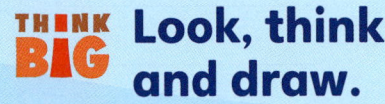

16 **Look at 15. Read and circle.**

1 A sundial uses **a shadow / clouds** to tell the time.

2 A sundial **works / doesn't work** at night.

3 The candle in a candle clock changes **height / color**.

4 People **use / don't use** hourglasses now.

5 A water clock uses water and **sand / cups** to tell the time.

17 **What is it? Choose and play a game.**

candle   cup   hourglass   sand   sundial   water clock

It uses the sun to tell the time.

A sundial!

You drink with it.

A cup!

PROJECT

18 **Make a Clock poster. Then present it to the class.**

This is a cuckoo clock. It uses a cuckoo to tell the time. It's eleven o'clock in this picture.

Cuckoo! Cuckoo!

19 Listen and read. Then say.

Journalist:	Who are you?
Steve Radcliff:	I'm Steve Radcliff.
Journalist:	What's your job?
Steve Radcliff:	I'm a teacher.
Journalist:	Where do you work?
Steve Radcliff:	In a school in London.
Journalist:	How do you get to work?
Steve Radcliff:	By train and bus.
Journalist:	When do you work?
Steve Radcliff:	I work from Monday through Friday and sometimes on Saturday.
Journalist:	How many students are in your class?
Steve Radcliff:	Thirty-five. It's enough for me!

 20 Read. Then circle the question words in **19**.

question word	possible answers	topic
who	*Steve Radcliff, my mom*	people
what	*job, table*	things
when	*on Saturday, every day*	time
where	*at home, in a school*	place
how	*by car, by bus*	manner
how many	*three, thirty-five*	number

do questions: Where **do** you **work**? How **does** he **get** to work?
am/is/are questions: Who **are** you? Where**'s** your coat?

21 **Read and match.**

1 Who is she?
2 What does she do?
3 Where does she sell the stories?
4 How do you get to town?
5 When is the bookstore open?

a In the bookstore.
b She writes stories.
c By bus.
d Jane Bowling.
e Every day.

22 **Read and circle.**

1 **A: What / Where** is that?   **B:** It's Marisa's T-shirt.

2 **A: When / How many** is your party? **B:** Today!

3 **A: How / How many** dolls do you have?   **B:** Only one.

4 **A: How / What** do you play soccer? **B:** You kick a ball.

5 **A: When / Where** are you going?   **B:** My grandma's house.

23 **Write. Use question words and do, is, or are.**

1 A: _____ ____ your friends?   **B:** Bella, James, and Sam.

2 A: _____ ____ you live?   **B:** In the United States.

3 A: _____ ____ your favorite food?   **B:** Pasta.

4 A: _____ ____ you go to school?   **B:** By bike.

5 A: _____ ____ you have English lessons?   **B:** On Wednesday.

24 **Look at 23. Ask and answer for you.**

Who are your friends?   Sophie and Bill.

My Day

All around the world, children eat, play, and go to school, but some children have very different routines from others.

Bruno, Brazil

1 I get up at 6 o'clock and go to school from 7 o'clock to 12 o'clock. Then I go home for a big lunch with my family. In the afternoon, I play with my friends or go to a dance class. I love to dance! Dinner is at 8 o'clock. After that, I'm very tired, and I go to bed.

25 How many hours are you at school every day? Is it a long time?

26 Listen and read. Which day is like yours?

27 Look at **26**. Circle **T** for true and **F** for false.

1 Bruno goes to school in the afternoon. **T** **F**

2 Jun eats with her mom and dad in the evening. **T** **F**

3 Ali goes to bed in the afternoon. **T** **F**

THINK BIG Is a long school day good or bad? Why?

Jun, China

2   My school starts at 8 o'clock and finishes at 5 o'clock, but we have recess for two hours at lunchtime. I have dinner with my mom and dad at 7 o'clock. When I finish my homework, I like to watch TV.

Ali, Egypt

3   I go to school from Sunday to Thursday because Friday is a holiday here. Classes start at 8 o'clock. At 10 o'clock we have recess, and school finishes at 3 o'clock. I play with my sisters in the afternoon, and we go to bed at 9 o'clock.

28 Look and complete. Then write.

My Perfect School Day

activity	time
get up	
	before school
start school	
	at recess
finish school	
	after school
have dinner	
go to bed	

I get up at seven o'clock. I have breakfast before school.

 **133**

29 **Listen and number in order. Then say.**

a

I get dressed quickly
and eat breakfast.

b

I always get to school
on time.

c

I get my backpack ready
the night before school.

d

I get up early on
school days.

30 **Tell your partner how you get to school on time.
Do the actions.**

I get up early
on school days.

 **THINK BIG** We all come to school at the same
time. Why is this good?
What other things is it good to be
on time for? Why?

134

 31 **Listen, look, and repeat.**

1 ch   **2** tch   **3** sh

135

 32 **Listen and find. Then say.**

wi**tch**   **ch**in   **sh**ip

fi**sh**   rich

136

 33 **Listen and blend the sounds.**

1 ch-o-p   chop   **2** sh-e   she

3 m-a-tch match   **4** l-u-n-ch lunch

5 d-i-sh   dish   **6** w-a-tch watch

137

 34 **Underline ch, tch, and sh. Then listen and chant.**

Watch the witch,
She's having lunch!
Fries and fish
From a dish!

Fishy Corner

35 **Play the Silly Sentences game.**

First, write times on cards. Then write daily activities on other cards.

Now work in groups. Make two piles of cards. Take turns. Turn over one card from each pile and read a silly sentence.

I go to bed at three o'clock.

That's silly! When do you really go to bed?

I go to bed at eight o'clock.

Now I'm going to make a sentence.

36 **Look and write. What time is it?**

1 It's _____. **2** It's _____. **3** It's _____.

4 It's _____. **5** It's _____. **6** It's _____.

37 **Read and match.**

1 Where is	**a** you eat for dinner?
2 Who are	**b** do you wake up?
3 What do	**c** Jane's book?
4 When	**d** the actors?

38 **Find and write the words.**

1 An _____ uses sand to tell the time. (galhossru)

2 A _____ uses the sun to tell the time. (ladsuin)

3 A water _____ uses water to tell the time. (ccolk)

4 We use clocks and _____ to tell the time. (swtaech)

I Can

☐ talk about times and daily activities.

☐ ask questions.

☐ talk about different ways of telling time.

Do I Know It?

1 **Think about it. Look and circle. Practice.**

🙂 I know this. 😕 I don't know this.

| 1 | | 🙂 😕 | p. 58 |

| 2 | | 🙂 😕 | p. 74 |

| 3 | | 🙂 😕 | p. 90 |

| 4 | | 🙂 😕 | p. 94 |

| **5** He wants to buy a book. | 🙂 😕 | p. 62 |

| **6** Is there a movie theater near here? Yes, there is./No, there isn't. | 🙂 😕 | p. 63 |

| **7** How much is that pen? It's two dollars and fifty cents. | 🙂 😕 | p. 66 |

| **8** What do you want to be? I want to be a pilot. | 🙂 😕 | p. 78 |

| **9** I want to be a doctor because I love science. | 🙂 😕 | p. 82 |

| **10** I think she's a nurse because she looks kind. | 🙂 😕 | p. 82 |

| **11** When does she get up? She gets up at seven o'clock. | 🙂 😕 | p. 94 |

| **12** Who's that? Where are you? What's your job? | 🙂 😕 | p. 98 |

2 **Get ready.**

A Look, listen, and write.

> artist   athlete   do   does   teacher   where

Charlie: Hey, Linda, what do you want to be?

Linda: I want to be an ¹_____ because I love sports.

Charlie: Really? What ²_____ your sister want to be?

Linda: She wants to be an ³_____.

Charlie: Why?

Linda: Well, my uncle is an artist. It's his job.

Charlie: ⁴_____ does he work?

Linda: He works at home. He draws pictures for books. What ⁵_____ you want to be, Charlie?

Charlie: I want to be a ⁶_____ because I like school!

B Talk about what you want to be. Say why.

What do you want to be?

I want to be a vet. I like animals.

3 Get set.

✂ **STEP 1** Cut out the cards on page 183.

📋 **STEP 2** Put the cards on your desk. Mix the cards up.
Now you're ready to **Go!**

4 Go!

A Take turns with a partner. Pick up a card. Continue until you find a matching card. Read your cards aloud.

I want to buy a book.

Is there a bookstore near here?

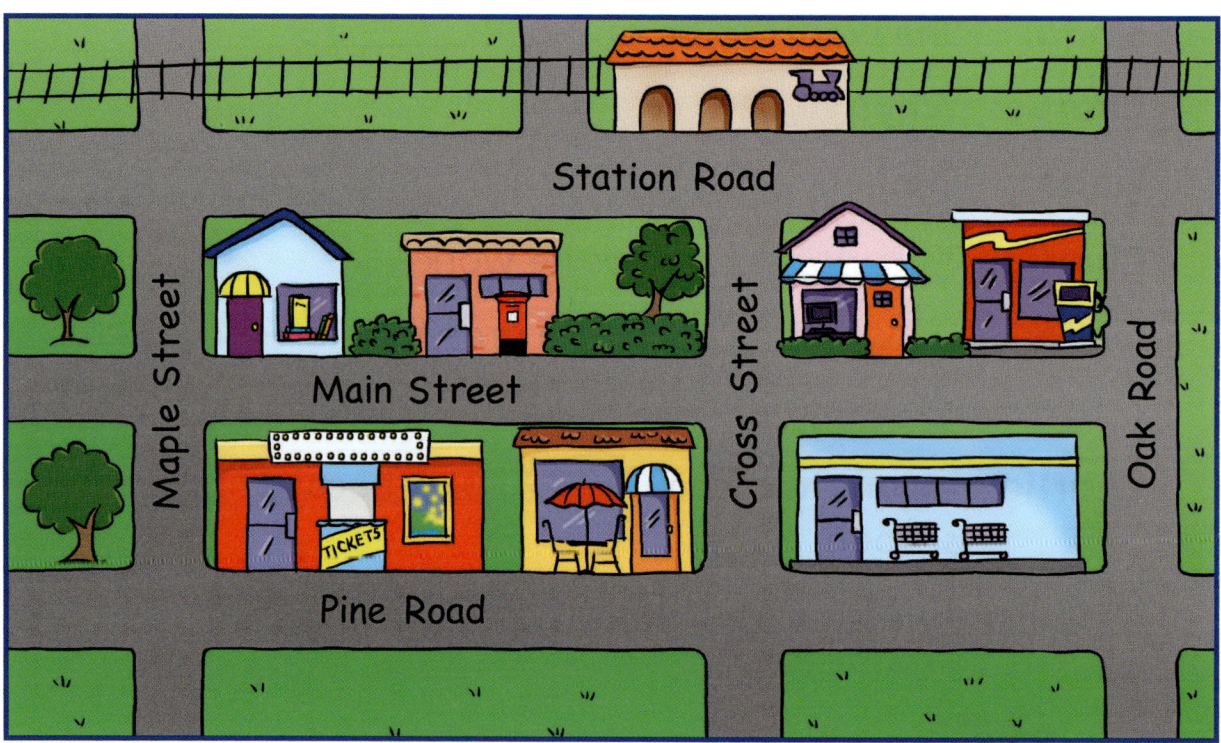

B Hold up one card at a time and find it on the map.
Ask and answer.

Where's the bookstore?

It's on Main Street.

5 Write or draw.

All About Me

What do you want to be? Why?	What time do you start school?
Where's your school?	When do you go to bed?

Do I Know It Now?

6 Think about it.

A Go to page **106**. Look and circle again.

B Check (✔).

☐ I can start the next unit.

☐ I can ask my teacher for help and then start the next unit.

☐ I can practice and then start the next unit.

7 Rate this Checkpoint. Color the stars.

 easy  hard

 fun not fun

Units 4–6 Exam Preparation

– Part A –

 Listen and check (✔) the box. There is one example.

Where is the bookstore?

 **A** ☐    **B** ✔    **C** ☐

1 What does Kim want to buy?

 **A** ☐    **B** ☐    **C** ☐

2 How does Nick go to school?

 **A** ☐    **B** ☐    **C** ☐

3 What time is it now?

 **A** ☐    **B** ☐    **C** ☐

4 Who's Anna's dad?

 **A** ☐    **B** ☐    **C** ☐

5 What time does the boy get up?

 **A** ☐    **B** ☐    **C** ☐

– Part B –

Read this. Choose a word from the box. Write the correct word next to numbers 1–5. There is one example.

Lucy wakes up at _____ *eight* _____ o'clock every day. She gets dressed and eats ¹_____ in the kitchen. Then she brushes her ²_____. Lucy plays the ³_____ all day. Then she ⁴_____ out. She doesn't like cooking. She eats dinner in a ⁵_____ next to her house.

What's Lucy's job?
She's a singer.

example			
eight	restaurant	chef	teeth
goes	breakfast	guitar	bus stop

My Favorite Food

141

1 Listen, look, and say.

1 bananas

2 apples

3 strawberries

4 tomatoes

5 carrots

6 potatoes

7 oranges

8 mangoes

9 cheese

10 yogurt

11 vegetables

12 sandwiches

13 burgers

14 snack

15 meat

142

2 Listen, find, and say.

3 Play a game.

4 **Listen and sing. Then look at 1 and find.**

Let's Eat Lunch!

It's twelve o'clock.
Let's eat lunch.
Do you like bananas?
I like them for lunch!

Do you like tomatoes?
Yes, I do. I like tomatoes. I really do.
Do you like potatoes?
Yes, I do. I like potatoes, too. Do you?

Meat and fruit,
Vegetables and snacks,
I like them all.
Can I have more, please?

Have some fries
And a burger, too.
Let's share some ice cream.
I like eating lunch with you!

5 **Listen, match, and write.**

I like _____. I like _____. I like _____.

1    2    3

a    b    c

6 **Look at 1. Ask and answer.**

Do you like bananas?

Yes, I do. I like bananas.

THINK BIG **Which pictures show fruit?**
Which pictures show vegetables?

147

7 Listen and read. Does Dan like apples?

Do You Like Fruit?

1

It's four o'clock, boys. Do you want a snack?

Yes, please, Dad.

2

There's fruit. Does Dan like fruit?

Yes, he does.

3

But I don't like bananas.

Jamie doesn't like bananas, either.

4

Do you like mangoes?

Yes, I do. I like mangoes.

8 **Look at the story. Write yes or no.**

1 Does Dan like fruit? _____

2 Does Jamie like bananas? _____

3 Does Dan like mangoes? _____

4 Do the boys like pie? _____

5 Is it a banana pie? _____

THINK BIG **What fruit do you like?**
What dishes can you make with fruit?

148

9 Listen. Help Jamie and Jenny make sentences.

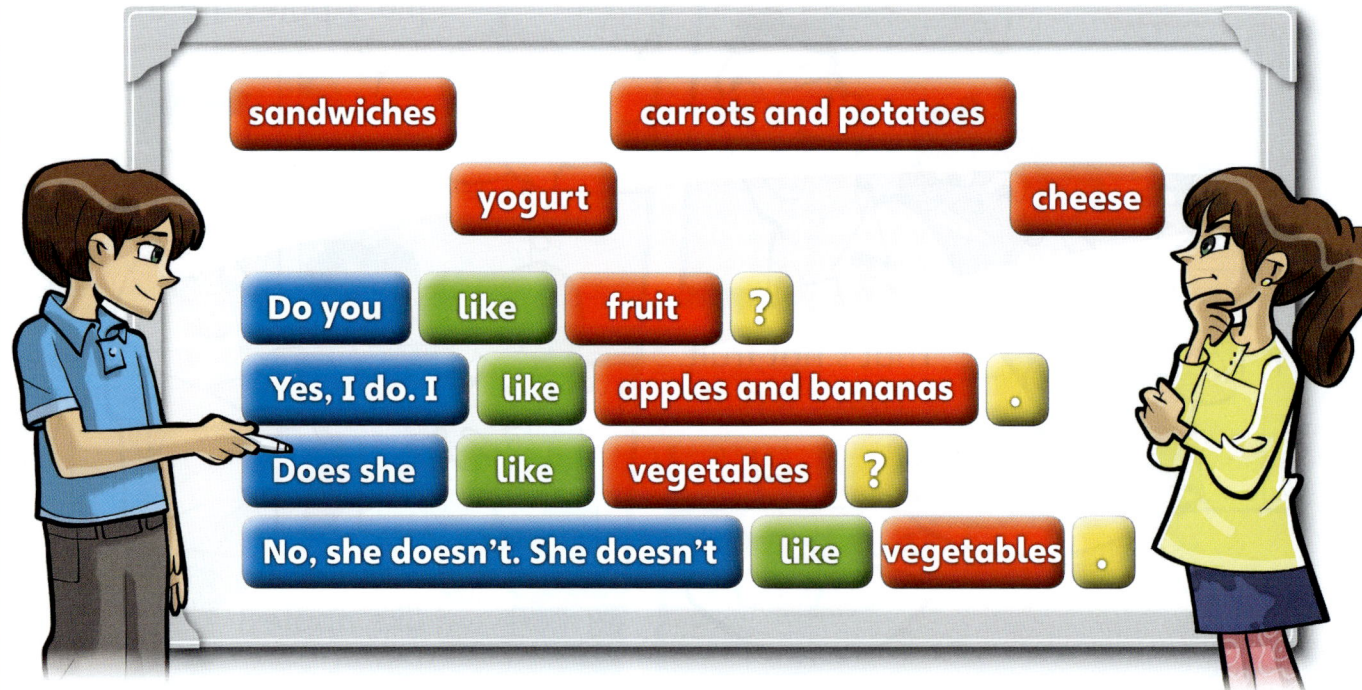

sandwiches   carrots and potatoes

yogurt   cheese

Do you | like | fruit | ?

Yes, I do. I | like | apples and bananas | .

Does she | like | vegetables | ?

No, she doesn't. She doesn't | like | vegetables | .

10 Look and write. Then answer.

1 _____ she like strawberries?
Yes, she _____. She _____ strawberries.

2 _____ he like tomatoes?
No, he _____. He _____ tomatoes.

3 _____ they like sandwiches?
Yes, they _____. They _____ sandwiches.

4 Do _____ like oranges?
_____, I _____. I _____
oranges.

150

11 Listen and stick. Then say.

1

2

3

4

12 Look at 11. Ask and answer.

Do you like strawberries?

No, I don't. I like apples.

13 Draw and write. Do you like vegetables?

_____

_____

_____

language practice (*Do you like fruit? Yes, I do.*) Unit 7 **117**

Look at the pictures. Which snacks can you name?

151

 Look, listen, and read. Then circle.

> **CONTENT WORDS**
> diabetes   disease   fat   healthy   heart
> label   salt   sugar   too much   unhealthy

Healthy and Unhealthy Snacks

Healthy food helps us grow and keeps us from getting sick. Some snacks are healthy, but others are not very healthy. Unhealthy snacks have too much sugar, fat, or salt.

1   Sugar

Sugar gives us energy, but when we don't use all that energy, it makes us fatter. Sugar is bad for our teeth and can give us diabetes. Candy has a lot of sugar.

2   Fat

Like sugar, fat gives us energy. When we eat too much of it, it stays in our body and makes us fatter. It can give us heart disease. Chocolate has a lot of fat.

3   Salt

Salt doesn't make us fatter, but too much of it can give us heart disease. Potato chips have a lot of salt.

Many snacks have labels that say how much sugar, fat, and salt is in them. Your mom or dad can help you read the labels and choose healthy snacks.

candy:
a lot of **sugar / salt**
chocolate:
a lot of **fat / salt**
potato chips:
a lot of **sugar / salt**

THINK BIG **Which snacks in the pictures are healthy? Which are unhealthy?**

16 **Look at 15. Read and match.**

1 Healthy food
2 Sugar and fat
3 Fat and salt
4 Too much sugar
5 Labels

a give us energy.
b is bad for our teeth.
c tell us how much fat, sugar, and salt is in snacks.
d helps us grow.
e can give us heart disease.

17 **Look. Then ask and answer.**

	fries	cakes	strawberries
sugar	★	★ ★ ★	★
fat	★ ★ ★	★ ★ ★	★
salt	★ ★ ★	★	★

Do fries have a lot of sugar?

No, they don't.

PROJECT

18 **Make a Healthy and Unhealthy Snacks poster. Then present it to the class.**

Unhealthy

a lot of fat and salt

a lot of fat and sugar

Healthy

not much fat, sugar, or salt

This salad is a healthy snack. It doesn't have much fat, sugar, or salt.

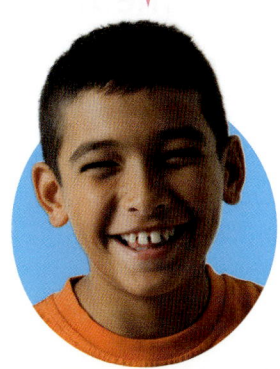

153

19 **Listen and read. Then say.**

Mom: Do you want some pasta for dinner, Ella?

Ella: Yes, please. And before that, can I have some fruit?

Mom: Sure. You can have an apple or a pear...

Ella: No, thanks, but I want some strawberries and some blueberries.

Mom: OK. You're eating a very healthy snack!

Ella: No, I'm not eating the food, Mom. I'm making a picture with it.

Mom: Oh, Ella! That looks amazing!

20 **Read. Then circle a, an and some in 19.**

Countable	Uncountable
• Apple, snack, and book are countable. • We can count these things (1 apple, 2 apple**s**, 3 apple**s**...). • We use **a/an/some** with these words.	• Pasta and water are uncountable. • We can't count these things (pasta, water...). • These words don't change. • We use **some** with these words.

21 **Circle the things you can count.**

1 meat   **2** milk   **3** carrot   **4** salt

5 cookie   **6** sugar   **7** sandwich   **8** potato

22 **Read and circle.**

1 **Joe:** Can I have **a** / **some** juice, please?

 Dad: Sorry, no, but you can have **a** / **some** water.

2 **Dad:** Do you want **a** / **some** burger for dinner?

 Joe: Yes, please. Can I have **an** / **some** orange for dessert?

23 **Read and write a, an, or some.**

Tim: I want ¹_____ meat, please. Can I have
 ²_____ big potato, too?

Waiter: Sure. And what about dessert? Do you want
 ³_____ orange?

Tim: No, thanks. I want ⁴_____ banana.

24 **Look. Choose three things. Then ask and answer.**

Do you want some cheese? No, thanks.

Do you want a cookie? Yes, please.

Where Fruit Comes From

watermelon

pineapple

Fruit is a very healthy snack. But where does it come from?

1   Watermelons come from South Africa. Turkey and China also grow a lot of watermelons, and they're very popular in Japan. In Japan they don't only have round watermelons. They have square ones, too!

25 Look at the fruit. Which do you like to eat?

154

26 Listen and read. Then match.

1 Pineapples   a South Africa

2 Watermelons   b China

3 Avocados   c South America

4 Kiwis   d Mexico

THINK BIG Supermarkets sell fruit from around the world. How do you know where it comes from?

kiwi

2   Pineapples grow in tropical countries, such as in South America. There are a lot of pineapple plants in the Philippines, and people there make fabric for clothes from pineapple leaves.

3   Kiwis are China's national fruit! They come from China, but now they grow in many parts of the world, like Italy and New Zealand. Their skin is ugly, but inside they're beautiful.

4   Many avocados come from Mexico, but they're popular all over the world. In Indonesia, people make a sweet drink with avocado, milk, sugar, and sometimes chocolate.

avocado

27   Look at 26. Read and write.

| avocados   kiwis   pineapples   watermelons |

1 You can eat _____, and the leaves are useful, too.
2 _____ can be round or square.
3 _____ are a national fruit.
4 New Zealand grows a lot of _____.
5 People make a sweet drink with _____.
6 _____ are popular in Japan.

155

28   Listen and say true or false. Then play a game.

Pineapples come from South Africa.

False! They come from Brazil.

Listen and number. Then write and say.

a

b

c

d

apple
carrots
chips
cookie

I want an _____, please.

No _____ for me, thanks.

Just one _____, please.

I like _____.

30 **Look and circle. Then look at 29 and role-play.**

1

healthy / unhealthy

2

healthy / unhealthy

3

healthy / unhealthy

4

healthy / unhealthy

5

healthy / unhealthy

6

healthy / unhealthy

 I want a carrot, please.

 No chocolate for me, thanks.

THINK BIG **What healthy food did you eat today?**
What unhealthy food did you eat today?

158

31 **Listen, look, and repeat.**

1 ee   **2** ie

159

32 **Listen and find. Then say.**

sheep   **pie**   **bee**   **tie**

160

33 **Listen and blend the sounds.**

1 f-ee-t   feet   **2** l-ie   lie

3 s-ee   see   **4** f-l-ie-s flies

5 ch-ee-se cheese   **6** c-r-ie-d cried

161

34 **Underline ee and ie. Then listen and chant.**

"See the cheese!"
Cried the bees.
"See the pies!"
Cried the flies.

35 **Play the What Do You Like? game.**

1 Circle yes for the foods you like. Circle no for the foods you don't like.
2 Guess what your partner likes. Circle.
3 Your partner says what he or she likes. Check (✓) your correct guesses.

	YOU		YOUR PARTNER		CORRECT?
1 carrots	yes	no	yes	no	
2 cheese	yes	no	yes	no	
3 tomatoes	yes	no	yes	no	
4 mangoes	yes	no	yes	no	
5 oranges	yes	no	yes	no	
6 burgers	yes	no	yes	no	
7 sandwiches	yes	no	yes	no	
8 meat	yes	no	yes	no	
9 strawberries	yes	no	yes	no	
10 potatoes	yes	no	yes	no	

Greg, do you like carrots?

Greg likes carrots. He doesn't like cheese.

Yes, I do.

36 **Tell the class what your partner likes and doesn't like.**

37 **Look and write. Use a, an, and some.**

1 She's eating _____ cookie.

2 They're eating _____ sandwiches.

3 He's drinking _____ milk.

4 He's eating _____ ice cream.

38 **Find and write the words.**

1 _____ come from Africa. (meWtalnosre)

2 _____ come from Mexico. (sadvoAco)

3 _____ come from China. (wiiKs)

4 _____ come from South America. (sipplPneae)

I Can

☐ **talk about food.**

☐ **talk about healthy and unhealthy food.**

☐ **say where fruit comes from.**

unit 8

Wild Animals

1 Listen, look, and say.

1 giraffe

2 hippo

3 kangaroo

4 cheetah

5 polar bear

6 zebra

7 parrot

8 monkey

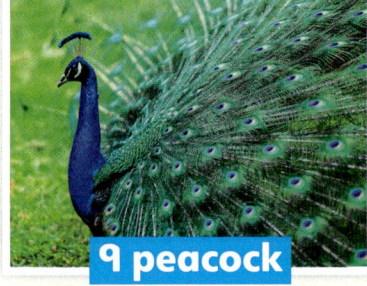
9 peacock

10 elephant

11 crocodile

12 snake

164
2 Listen, find, and say. **3** Play a game.

4 Listen and sing. Then look at 1 and find.

To the Zoo!

I really like animals!
Do you like them, too?
That's why I'm so happy.
We're going to the zoo!

A kangaroo can jump.
A monkey can jump, too.
Crocodiles can chase
And swim.
And you, what can you do?

A giraffe can't fly or jump up high.
An elephant can't climb trees.
Fish can't run, and hippos can't fly.
Come and see them.
Oh, yes, please!

Now it's time to say goodbye
To every animal here.
But we can come back
And see them every year!

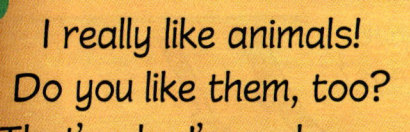

 5 Listen and say true or false.

6 Look at 1. Ask and answer.

Do you like cheetahs?

Yes, I do! Cheetahs can run.

THINK BIG Which animals can chase other animals? Which animals can climb trees?

169

7 **Listen and read. What animals does Jamie like?**

8 Look. Circle can or can't.

1 Monkeys **can / can't** climb trees.
2 Monkeys **can / can't** jump.
3 Hippos **can / can't** climb trees.
4 Hippos **can / can't** jump.
5 Hippos **can / can't** eat a lot.
6 Jamie **can / can't** eat a lot.

THINK BIG **What animals can swim, run, and eat fish?**
What animals can't fly or climb trees?

9 **Listen. Help Jamie and Jenny make sentences.**

a crocodile   giraffes   peacocks

swim   climb trees   fly

Can a kangaroo jump ?

Yes, it can .

Can snakes run ?

No, they can't .

10 **Look and write. Then draw and write.**

1 _____ a zebra see at night?
Yes, _____.

2 _____ cheetahs run?
Yes, _____.

3 _____ a giraffe climb trees?
No, _____.

4 _____
_____

171

11 Listen and stick. Then write.

elephants   kangaroos   monkeys   snakes

1 Can _____ climb trees?

2 Can _____ run?

3 Can _____ play?

4 Can _____ fly?

12 Look at 11. Ask and answer.

Can monkeys climb trees?

Yes, they can.

13 Write and draw. Then say.

_____

_____

_____

14 Look at the pictures. Which animals can you name?

172

15 Look, listen, and read. Then circle.

CONTENT WORDS

cover   desert   forest   fox   jungle
lizard   ocean   raccoon   seal   whale

Animal Habitats

A habitat is the place where an animal lives.

1   The **forest** is a cool dark habitat with a lot of trees. Deer, raccoons, and foxes live there. Forests cover ¹ **8% / 28%** of the planet.

2   ² **6% / 60%** of our planet is **desert**. It's hot in the day and cold at night. There isn't much rain, so it's very dry, and there aren't many plants. Lizards and snakes live there.

3   The **ocean** covers ³ **21% / 71%** of our planet, and the water in it is salty. Many kinds of fish live in the ocean. Other animals live there, too, like whales and seals.

4   It's hot in the **jungle**, and it rains a lot. Monkeys, colorful birds, and butterflies live there. There are tigers, too! The jungle covers only ⁴ **2% / 12%** of the planet, but 50% of all plant and animal species live there.

THINK BIG   Which animal habitats are in your country? Which animals live there?

16 **Look at 15. Read and match.**

1
Foxes

2
Monkeys

3 Snakes

4
Whales

a live in the ocean.
c live in the forest.

b live in the desert.
d live in the jungle.

17 **Think of an animal. Ask and answer.**

Can it swim? — Yes.

Does it live in the ocean? — Yes.

Is it a whale? — Yes.

PROJECT

18 **Make an Animal Habitats poster. Then present it to the class.**

Tigers live in the jungle. It's hot and wet there.

content connection (animal habitats) Unit 8 **135**

174

19 **Listen and read. Then say.**

Jane: Dad has a nice new camera. His pictures from the zoo are great!

Sam: Can I see them?

Jane: Sure! Look at this giraffe with its long black tongue.

Sam: It's really cool! And I love that beautiful young polar bear.

Jane: Me, too, but my favorite animal is this funny green frog with big, red eyes. It's amazing!

20 **Read. Then circle the describing words in 19.**

Putting describing words in order
1 opinion   2 size/shape   3 age   4 color
a nice new camera ✓ (a new nice camera ✗)
a long black tongue
a beautiful young polar bear
a funny green frog
big red eyes

21 **Look at 20. Read and ✔ or ✗.**

1 a long black scarf ☐

2 a black long scarf ☐

3 big red boots ☐

4 a green funny bird ☐

5 new nice shoes ☐

22 **Look and write.**

| beautiful | blue | cool | funny | gray | long |
| nice | old | short | small | white | young |

opinion	size/shape	age	color
amazing	big	new	yellow

23 **Read, order, and write.**

1 The _____, _____ (brown, tall) giraffe is eating the _____, _____ (nice, green) leaves.

2 The _____, _____ (blue, old) peacock has a _____, _____ (green, beautiful) tail.

3 The _____, _____ (gray, big) kangaroo is carrying a _____, _____ (beautiful, young) baby.

24 **Choose the correct clues and draw a monster.**

My monster has...

two big, green heads. ☐
two red, small heads. ☐
four long, funny hands. ☐
four nice, small hands. ☐
three new, short shoes. ☐
three long, old shoes. ☐

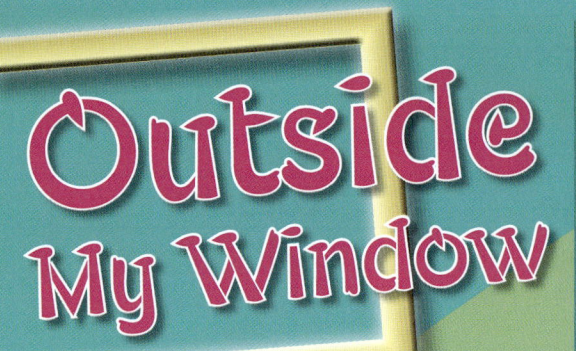

On this website, kids around the world can share stories and pictures about the amazing animals that live near their homes. Let's take a look.

1   This is a koala. Koalas come from Australia, and so do I! This one lives in the gum tree outside my bedroom window. She sleeps a lot, but when she isn't sleeping, she's very interesting. She's very slow, and she eats and eats.

Vincent, Australia

a

25 **Look at the pictures. Then match.**

It can make snowballs.   It sleeps a lot.   It's a pet.

175
26 **Listen and read. Then check your answers in 25.**

THINK BIG **Can you see these animals in your country? Where? Which animals are good pets? Why?**

2   Every day when I wake up, I see a friendly face in the field outside my window. His name is Papi, and he's a llama. He's not a wild llama, he's a family pet. He can jump very high.

Angela, Peru

3   I can see some wonderful animals near my home. They're snow monkeys, and they live in the forest. They like to make snowballs. I can see them from our car window, but I don't go too close. They aren't pets.

Kyoko, Japan

27 **Look at 26. Read and match.**

Animal	Country	Where does it live?	What does it do?
llama	Peru	a tree	makes snowballs
koala	Japan	the forest	sleeps a lot
snow monkey	Australia	a field	jumps high

28 **Complete the chart about an animal that lives near you. Then ask and answer.**

What animal is it?	
Where does it live?	
What does it do?	

What animal is it?   A fox.

29 **Listen and number. Then say.**

a

I think
peacocks are
beautiful.

b

Monkeys are
so smart.

c

Giraffes are
amazing.
Their necks
are so long.

d

Elephants are
very strong.

30 **Look at 29. Ask and answer.**

amazing   beautiful   smart   strong

What animal do you like?

I like parrots.
They're so beautiful.

THINK BIG **What is your favorite animal? Why?**

31 **Listen, look, and repeat.**

1 OU   **2** OW

32 **Listen and find. Then say.**

cow

soup

owl

You

you

33 **Listen and blend the sounds.**

1 g-r-ou-p   group   **2** t-ow-n   town

3 t-ou-c-a-n   toucan   **4** c-l-ow-n   clown

5 d-ow-n   down   **6** s-ou-p   soup

34 **Underline ou and ow. Then listen and chant.**

An owl went
Down to town
To see a group
Of toucans
Drinking soup.

35 **Play the What Animal Am I? game.**

Step 1. Write the name of an animal on a sticky note. Don't show your partner.

Step 2. Stick your note on your partner's forehead. Your partner asks you questions and guesses the animal.

Can I fly?

No, you can't.

Can I swim?

Yes, you can.

Am I black?

No, you're white.

Am I a polar bear?

Yes, you are.

Step 3. Now play with other partners.

36 **Look and** ✔.

1 a short black skirt ☐
    a black short skirt ☐

2 a blue cool jacket ☐
    a cool blue jacket ☐

3 long nice pants ☐
    nice long pants ☐

4 new red boots ☐
    red new boots ☐

5 small funny gloves ☐
    funny small gloves ☐

6 old green shorts ☐
    green old shorts ☐

37 **Read and circle.**

1 Whales live in **jungles** / **oceans**.

2 Monkeys live in **jungles** / **deserts**.

3 Fish live in **forests** / **oceans**.

4 Foxes live in **jungles** / **forests**.

I Can
☐ **describe animals.**
☐ **talk about where animals live.**
☐ **talk about appreciating animals.**

unit 9 Fun All Year

1 Listen, look, and say.

January
SUN	MON	TUE	WED	THU	FRI	SAT
1	2	3	4	5	6	7
8	9	10	11	12	13	14
15	16	17	18	19	20	21
22	23	24	25	26	27	28
29	30	31				

February
SUN	MON	TUE	WED	THU	FRI	SAT
		1	2	3	4	
5	6	7	8	9	10	11
12	13	14	15	16	17	18
19	20	21	22	23	24	25
26	27	28	29			

March
SUN	MON	TUE	WED	THU	FRI	SAT
			1	2	3	
4	5	6	7	8	9	10
11	12	13	14	15	16	17
18	19	20	21	22	23	24
25	26	27	28	29	30	31

April
SUN	MON	TUE	WED	THU	FRI	SAT
1	2	3	4	5	6	7
8	9	10	11	12	13	14
15	16	17	18	19	20	21
22	23	24	25	26	27	28
29	30					

May
SUN	MON	TUE	WED	THU	FRI	SAT
	1	2	3	4	5	
6	7	8	9	10	11	12
13	14	15	16	17	18	19
20	21	22	23	24	25	26
27	28	29	30	31		

June
SUN	MON	TUE	WED	THU	FRI	SAT
					1	2
3	4	5	6	7	8	9
10	11	12	13	14	15	16
17	18	19	20	21	22	23
24	25	26	27	28	29	30

July
SUN	MON	TUE	WED	THU	FRI	SAT
1	2	3	4	5	6	7
8	9	10	11	12	13	14
15	16	17	18	19	20	21
22	23	24	25	26	27	28
29	30	31				

August
SUN	MON	TUE	WED	THU	FRI	SAT
		1	2	3	4	
5	6	7	8	9	10	11
12	13	14	15	16	17	18
19	20	21	22	23	24	25
26	27	28	29	30	31	

September
SUN	MON	TUE	WED	THU	FRI	SAT
						1
2	3	4	5	6	7	8
9	10	11	12	13	14	15
16	17	18	19	20	21	22
23	24	25	26	27	28	29
30						

October
SUN	MON	TUE	WED	THU	FRI	SAT
	1	2	3	4	5	6
7	8	9	10	11	12	13
14	15	16	17	18	19	20
21	22	23	24	25	26	27
28	29	30	31			

November
SUN	MON	TUE	WED	THU	FRI	SAT
				1	2	3
4	5	6	7	8	9	10
11	12	13	14	15	16	17
18	19	20	21	22	23	24
25	26	27	28	29	30	

December
SUN	MON	TUE	WED	THU	FRI	SAT
						1
2	3	4	5	6	7	8
9	10	11	12	13	14	15
16	17	18	19	20	21	22
23	24	25	26	27	28	29
30	31					

2 Listen, find, and say. **3** Play a game.

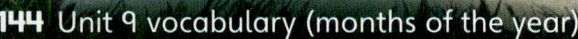

4 Listen and chant. Then look at 1 and find.

I Like July!

July is my favorite month.
I like August, too.
I'm happy and on vacation,
There is so much to do!

I also like September.
That's when I start school.
I'm so excited, aren't you?
My friends will be there, too!

I don't like December.
It's very, very cold.
But then it is my birthday, too.
This year, I'm eight years old!

188

5 Listen and write the month.

1 _____ 2 _____ 3 _____

6 Look at 1. Ask and answer.

What's your favorite month?

I like May.

THINK BIG Which months are vacation months at school?

7 Listen and read. When is Jamie's birthday?

5 I never go to school. I always have a big party!

6 And Mom always makes a big chocolate cake! August is my favorite month!

8 **Look at the story. Circle.**

1 Jenny's favorite month is **January** / **December**.

2 Dan goes swimming in **January** / **August**.

3 Jamie's favorite month is **August** / **May**.

4 Jenny always goes on vacation in **December** / **November**.

5 Dan never goes on vacation in **August** / **December**.

6 Jamie always has a party in **April** / **August**.

THINK BIG **When do you go on vacation?**
I always go on vacation in _____.
I never go on vacation in _____.

9 Listen. Help Jamie and Jenny make sentences.

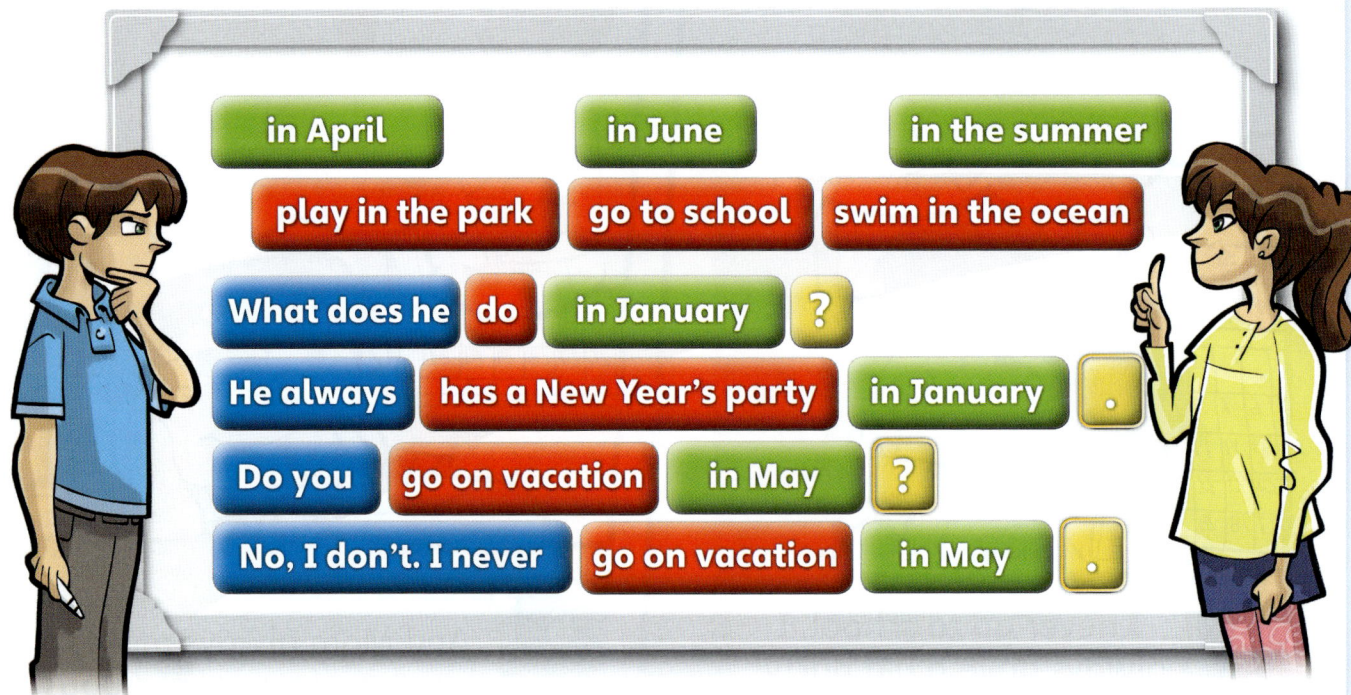

in April   in June   in the summer

play in the park   go to school   swim in the ocean

What does he **do** in January **?**

He always has a New Year's party in January **.**

Do you go on vacation in May **?**

No, I don't. I never go on vacation in May **.**

10 Write and circle.

1 What does she do in the summer? Does she play tennis?
Yes, she _____. She **always** / **never** plays tennis
in the summer.

2 What _____ you do in February? Do you go
on vacation?
No, we _____. We **always** / **never** go on vacation
in February.

3 Do they go to school in September?
Yes, they _____. They **always** / **never** go to
school in September.

4 Do you go to the park in the winter?
_____. I **always** / **never** go to the park
in the winter.

11 **Listen and stick. Then write the number.**

192

a
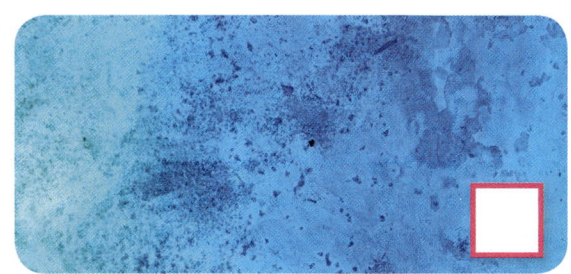

We always swim in the ocean.

b

We always go to my grandpa's house.

c

We always go on vacation.

d

I always play soccer with my friends.

12 **Look at 11. Ask and answer.**

Do you go on vacation in April?

No, I don't. I never go on vacation in April.

13 **Write and draw. What do you do in the winter?**

I _____

_____

in the winter.

14 Look at pictures **a–d**. What are the people doing?

193

15 Look, listen, and read. When are the festivals? Number in order from January.

CONTENT WORDS

celebration   confetti   hang   pole   wish

Celebrating
Special Days

Every country has special days and exciting celebrations. Let's take a look at some of them.

a

People in England celebrate spring on May 1st. On **May Day**, people put flowers and ribbons on a special pole. Children hold the ribbons and dance around the pole.

b

Italy is famous for its **carnivals**. In February and March, there are parties in the streets. People wear masks, and children throw small pieces of paper called confetti.

In China, people celebrate the **Mid-Autumn Festival**. This festival happens in September or October when the moon is very big and bright. Children wear colorful masks and dance in the streets. They also eat sweet cakes called mooncakes.

c

In Japan, people celebrate the star festival, **Tanabata**. In July and August, people write wishes on paper. They hang the wishes on bamboo to make a "wish tree."

d

☐ May Day

☐ Mid-Autumn Festival

☐ Carnivals in Italy

☐ Tanabata

THINK BIG What celebrations does your country have? What do people do?

16 🗨 **Look at 15 and ✔.**

	May Day	Carnival	Mid-Autumn	Tanabata
wear masks				
eat special food				
dance				
make wishes				
throw paper				

17 🗨 **Look and say. Then ask your friends.**

Name	Favorite festival	When?

What's your favorite festival?

Independence Day.

When do you celebrate Independence Day?

In the summer.

PROJECT

18 🗨 **Make a Festivals poster. Then present it to the class.**

Winter

We celebrate Christmas in the winter.

We celebrate Christmas in the winter. We have parties and decorate our homes.

195

19 Listen and read. Then say.

Tom:	Hi, Tom. How are you?
Joe:	Great, thanks! I love winter vacations.
Tom:	What's the weather like there?
Joe:	It's snowing. It's very cold, but I like it. What's the weather like at home?
Tom:	It's raining. I hate days like this!
Joe:	What are you doing?
Tom:	I'm writing a story. In my story, it's always summer. It's always hot and sunny in the summer!

20 Read. Then circle the words in **19**.

It's **hot**.		It's **raining**.	
It's **cold**.		It's **snowing**.	
It's **sunny**.			

196

21 Listen and circle. Then listen and repeat.

1 London:  **2** Paris:

3 New York:  **4** Mexico City: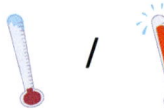

22 **Put the words in order. Then say.**

1 like | the weather | What's | there?
2 cold | It's | and rainy. | very
3 in the summer. | It's | hot | always
4 like it. | It's | but I | very cold,
5 sunny | today. | It's hot | and
6 What's | weather | the | in | like | New York?

23 **Look. Then ask and answer.**

Jan–Feb	Mar–Apr	May–Jun	Jul–Aug	Sep–Oct	Nov–Dec

24 **Imagine. Then draw and write.**

1 What month is it?
   It's _____.

2 What's the weather like?
   It's _____.

3 What are you doing?
   I'm _____.

New Year's Eve

People all over the world celebrate New Year's Eve on the night of December 31st. It's the last day of the year, and there are a lot of parties. But celebrations at midnight are very different in different places.

1 In Spain, people eat twelve grapes at twelve o'clock – one with every chime of the clock. People think that the grapes bring good luck for the next year. Then there are fireworks.

25 **Is New Year special in your country? What do you do?**

197
26 **Listen and read. Then match.**

1 Spain		**a** listen to something
2 Scotland		**b** sing a song
3 Japan		**c** eat fruit

THINK BIG **What do people in your country do when they want good luck? Do you think it works?**

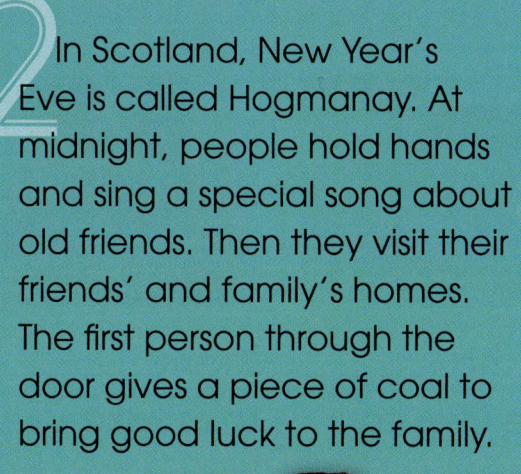

2 In Scotland, New Year's Eve is called Hogmanay. At midnight, people hold hands and sing a special song about old friends. Then they visit their friends' and family's homes. The first person through the door gives a piece of coal to bring good luck to the family.

3 In Japan, people eat a special noodle soup on New Year's Eve for good luck. They eat the soup and listen to a bell ring 108 times at midnight. They believe the bell takes away 108 bad things before the New Year.

27 **Look at 26. Circle T for true and F for false.**

1 People in Spain eat grapes on New Year's Eve.   T   F

2 In Scotland, singing a song brings good luck.   T   F

3 In Japan, people eat 108 noodles for good luck.   T   F

28 **Look, answer, and write.**

New Year's Eve in My Country
On New Year's Eve in ¹_____,
we wear ²_____. We eat
³_____. We celebrate
⁴_____ with ⁵_____.
At midnight, we ⁶_____.

1 Which country?
2 Ordinary clothes?
  Special clothes?
  What kind and color?
3 What foods?
4 Where?
5 Who?
6 What do you do?

199

29 **Listen and write the season. Then say.**

fall   spring   winter   summer

1

2

3

4

In the _____, they skate on ice.

In the _____, he rides his bike.

In the _____, she likes to swim.

In the _____, they rake leaves.

30 **Draw and write. What do you do in each season?**

1 In the summer, _____ _____.

2 In the winter, _____ _____.

31 **Look at 30. Ask and answer.**

What do you do in the winter?

In the winter, I do gymnastics.

TH NK BIG **What can you only do in the winter? Why?**
What can you only do in the summer? Why?

200

32 **Listen, look, and say.**

Aa	Bb	Cc	Dd	Ee
Ff	Gg	Hh	Ii	Jj
Kk	Ll	Mm	Nn	Oo
Pp	Qq	Rr	Ss	Tt
Uu	Vv	Ww	Xx	Yy	Zz

 201

33 **Listen, look, and chant. Can you find something starting with every letter of the alphabet?**

A, B, C, D, E, F, G.
I can see an ant and a bat. What can you see?
H, I, J, K, L, M, N, O, P.
I can see a lion and some ink. What can you see?
Q, R, S, T, U, V.
I can see a rat and a snake. What can you see?
W, X, Y, and Z.
Six yellow wolves and a zebra are what I see!

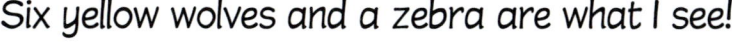

34 **Play the Months Lineup game.**

Step 1. Ask when your classmates' birthdays are. Then line up in order by month.

Step 2. Check the order with the class.

Step 3. Play the game again. Ask and answer. Then line up again by month.

1 What is your favorite month?
2 What is your favorite vacation?
3 When is your favorite school event?

35 Look and match.

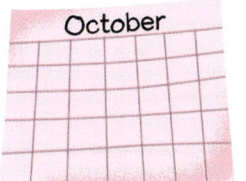
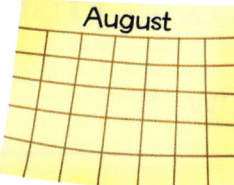

October   August   February   May

a    **b**    **c**   **d**

36 Write about you.

1 What do you do in the winter?

I always _____ in the winter.

I never _____ in the winter.

2 What do you do in the summer?

I always _____ in the summer.

I never _____ in the summer.

3 What do you do in the fall?

I always _____ in the fall.

I never _____ in the fall.

4 What do you do in the spring?

I always _____ in the spring.

I never _____ in the spring.

☐ talk about what I do each month.

☐ talk about the weather.

☐ talk about seasonal holidays.

1 **Think about it. Look and circle. Practice.**

😊 I know this.   😟 I don't know this.

1		😊 😟	p. 112
2		😊 😟	p. 128
3		😊 😟	p. 144
4		😊 😟	p. 145

5	Does she like fruit? Yes, she does./No, she doesn't.	😊 😟	p. 116
6	I want a pizza, some fries, and some salad.	😊 😟	p. 120
7	Can snakes jump? Yes, they can./No, they can't.	😊 😟	p. 132
8	I have a nice new jacket and cool brown shoes.	😊 😟	p. 136
9	What does he do in January? He always has a New Year's party in January.	😊 😟	p. 148
10	Do you go on vacation in the winter? Yes, we do./ No, we don't. We never go on vacation in the winter.	😊 😟	p. 149
11	What's the weather like? It's raining and cold.	😊 😟	p. 152

204

2 Get ready.

A Look, listen, and write.

| always | an | can | can't | never | pet | some |

Alan: That's a beautiful, green parrot. Is it yours?

Tess: Yes. His name is Crackers. He's my
¹_____. He's very smart. He
²_____ talk!

Alan: He can?

Tess: Yes, he can.

Alan: That's amazing! Look – I have ³
_____ apple and ⁴_____
nuts. Does he like fruit?

Tess: Yes, he does. He loves it!

Alan: Ha, ha.

Tess: He can sing, too.

Alan: Really?

Tess: Yes. He ⁵_____ sings
to me in the morning!

Alan: Wow. My cat is so boring. She
⁶_____ say anything,
and she ⁷_____ sings to me!

B Look at **A**. Ask and answer.

> What can Crackers do?

> What can't Alan's cat do?

> Does Crackers like fruit?

1
2
3
4
5
6
7
8
9

3 **Get set.**

STEP 1 Cut out the outline on page 185. Cut each card in half along the dotted line.

STEP 2 Sort the cards into two piles. Put the heads of the animals in one pile and the bodies in the other. Now you're ready to **Go!**

4 **Go!**

A Put one card from each of your piles together to make a funny animal.

B Talk about your funny animals. Ask and answer.

This is an elebra!

Can elebras climb trees?

No, they can't.

Do they like fruit?

Yes, they do. They like oranges and mangoes.

C Look at others' animals. Who has the same animal as you?

5 Write or draw.

All About Me

When is your birthday?	What's the weather like today?
What's your favorite month?	What do you always do in the summer?

Do I Know It Now?

6 **Think about it.**

A Go to page **160**. Look and circle again.

B Check (✔).

☐   I can ask my teacher for help.

☐   I can practice.

7 **Rate this Checkpoint. Color the stars.**

 easy    hard    fun    not fun

Units 7–9 Exam Preparation

– Part A –

 Read the question. Listen and write a name or a number. There are two examples.

Examples

What's the girl's name?	Grace
How old is she?	6

Questions

1 What's Grace's friend's name? _____

2 Which class are they in? _____

3 How many parrots does Grace have? _____

4 What's the name of Grace's favorite parrot? _____

5 How many children are there in Grace's class? _____

– Part B –

Look at the pictures and read the questions. Write one-word answers.

Examples

How many hippos are there? _____ one _____

Where's the crocodile? under a _____ tree _____

Questions

1 What's the crocodile doing? it's _____

2 Where's the monkey now? on the girl's _____

3 What's the monkey taking? an _____

4 How many children are looking at the parrot? _____

5 What can the parrot do? it can _____

Young Learners English Practice Starters: Listening A

– 5 questions –

 Listen and check (✓) the box. There is one example.

What's Alex doing?

A ☐

B ☑

C ☐

1 What's Jill doing?

A ☐

B ☐

C ☐

2 What's Ben doing?

A ☐

B ☐

C ☐

3 Where's Pat's jacket?

 **A** ☐

 **B** ☐

 **C** ☐

4 How many people are in the picture?

 **A**

 **B** ☐

 **C** ☐

5 What are Bill and Ann doing?

 **A** ☐

 **B** ☐

 **C** ☐

– 5 questions –

Listen. Then read the questions and write a name or a number. There are two examples.

Examples

What is the boy's name?   _Tom_

How old is he?   _10_

Questions

1 How old is Sara?   _____

2 How many books does Tom have?   _____

3 What's the cat's name?   _____

4 What's the dog's name?   _____

5 Where's the library?   on _____ Street

– 5 questions –

 Listen and draw lines. There is one example.

– 5 questions –

Look at the pictures. Look at the letters. Write the words.

Example

s w i n g

g w i n s

Questions

1

_ _ _ _ _ _ _ _

r e t m o c u p

2

_ _ _ _ _

d e s l i

3

_ _ _ _ _ _ _ _ _ _

t a s k e d r a b o

4

_ _ _ _ _ _

n e c l i p

5

_ _ _ _ _ _ _

r e t i c u p

– 5 questions –

**Look and read. Put a check (✓) or a cross (✗) in the box.
There are two examples.**

Examples

She's a doctor. ✔

This is a bus stop. ✗

Questions

1

This is a bookstore. ☐

2

She's a dancer. ☐

3

He's a teacher. ☐

4

This is a gas station. ☐

5

He's a singer. ☐

– 5 questions –

Read this. Choose a word from the box. Write the correct word next to numbers 1–5. There is one example.

A Zoo

I am a big place. A lot of animals live in me. The _elephant_ has big ears and a long trunk. The ¹_____ is a bird with a beautiful tail. The ²_____ is another beautiful bird. It likes talking. Then there are ³_____. They have long tails and live in my trees.

The ⁴_____ is a large, gray animal with small ears. It likes the water. And the ⁵_____ has a long neck and spots. What am I? I am a zoo.

example			
elephant	peacock	giraffe	hippo
kangaroo	monkeys	toucan	snake

Wordlist

Unit 1	Page
classroom	4
coloring	4
counting	4
cutting	4
gluing	4
listening	4
playing a game	4
using the computer	4
watching a DVD	4
writing	4
a hundred	10
equals	10
minus	10
plus	10
in a forest	14
in a garden	14
in the mountains	14
on a boat	14
take turns	16
bath	17
both	17
crocodile	17
math	17
mouth	17
path	17
teeth	17
then	17
thin	17
with	17

Unit 2	Page
climbing trees	20
doing gymnastics	20

flying kites	20
ice-skating	20
playing tennis	20
playing volleyball	20
riding my bike	20
skateboarding	20
like	21
love	21
playground	21
running	21
swing	21
together	22
team	23
bones	26
exercise	26
feet	26
fingers	26
jump	26
kick	26
move	26
muscles	26
strong	26
throw	26
weak	26
each side	32
helmet	32
in front of	32
knee pads	32
safely	32
slide	32
seesaw	32
bang	33
bank	33
ink	33

king	33
ring	33
sink	33
wing	33

Unit 3	Page
bathroom	36
bathtub	36
bed	36
bedroom	36
chair	36
closet	36
oven	36
couch	36
dresser	36
DVD player	36
fridge	36
kitchen	36
lamp	36
living room	36
table	36
TV	36
sink	36
glasses	37
in	37
keys	37
on	37
put on	37
aunt	38
cousin	38
uncle	38
quiet	39
behind	40
between	40

in front of	40	bus stop	58	taxi	68
next to	40	computer store	58	cross the street	70
under	40	gas station	58	last	70
phone	41	movie theater	58	left	70
burn	42	post office	58	pedestrian crossing	70
computer	42	restaurant	58	right	70
museum	42	shopping mall	58	second	70
new	42	supermarket	58	wait	70
oil	42	town	58	drive	71
old	42	train station	58	nail	71
screen	42	buy	59	oak	71
wheel	42	eat	59	rain	71
clay	46	far	59	sail	71
dry	46	letter	59	soap	71
electricity	46	map	59	tail	71
fuel	46	near	59	wear	71
household	46	send	59		
solar	46	first	60	**Unit 5**	**Page**
wet	46	hungry	60	actor	74
comfortable	47	wallet	61	artist	74
hammock	47	movie	62	athlete	74
dirty	48	boat	64	chef	74
dishes	48	canal	64	dancer	74
neat	48	fast	64	doctor	74
toy box	48	go to school by	64	dream job	74
washing machine	48	ground	64	pilot	74
cook	49	safe	64	singer	74
cool	49	slow	64	teacher	74
moon	49	street	64	vet	74
zoo	49	subway	64	writer	74
		design	68	carpenter	80
Unit 4	**Page**	famous	68	entertain	80
bank	58	long time ago	68	farmer	80
bookstore	58	sign	68	grow	80

Wordlist

hairdresser	80	come back	92	**Unit 7**	**Page**
nurse	80	in the afternoon	92	apples	112
produce	80	boring	93	bananas	112
provide	80	finish school	94	burgers	112
take care of	80	burn	96	carrots	112
waiter	80	candle	96	cheese	112
park ranger	84	cup	96	mangoes	112
rodeo rider	84	fall	96	meat	112
scuba diver	84	height	96	oranges	112
protect	85	hourglass	96	potatoes	112
art	86	sand	96	sandwiches	112
math	86	shadow	96	snack	112
music	86	sun	96	strawberries	112
science	86	sundial	96	tomatoes	112
set goals	86	tell the time	96	vegetables	112
study hard	86	use	96	yogurt	112
arm	87	water clock	96	fries	113
born	87	work	96	fruit	113
cart	87	routine	100	ice cream	113
corn	87	tired	100	share	113
letter	87	after school	101	pie	115
		at recess	101	chocolate	118
Unit 6	**Page**	before school	101	diabetes	118
o'clock	90	recess	101	disease	118
do my homework	91	early	102	fat	118
evening	91	on time	102	healthy	118
get dressed	91	quickly	102	heart	118
get up	91	ready	102	label	118
go out	91	chin	103	salt	118
go to bed	91	chop	103	sugar	118
sleep	91	rich	103	too much	118
start school	91	ship	103	unhealthy	118
stay in bed	91	witch	103	pineapple	122
watch	91			round	122

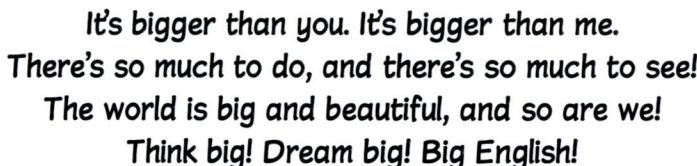

Big English Song

From the mountaintops to the bottom of the sea,
From a big blue whale to a baby bumblebee –
If you're big, if you're small, you can have it all,
And you can be anything you want to be!

It's bigger than you. It's bigger than me.
There's so much to do, and there's so much to see!
The world is big and beautiful, and so are we!
Think big! Dream big! Big English!

So in every land, from the desert to the sea,
We can all join hands and be one big family.
If we love, if we care, we can go anywhere!
The world belongs to everyone; it's ours to share.

It's bigger than you. It's bigger than me.
There's so much to do, and there's so much to see!
The world is big and beautiful, and so are we!
Think big! Dream big! Big English!

It's bigger than you. It's bigger than me.
There's so much to do, and there's so much to see!
The world is big and beautiful and waiting for me.
A one, two, three...
Think big! Dream big! Big English!

We want to go to the post office.

Is there a post office near here?

I want to buy a book.

Is there a bookstore near here?

My mom wants to eat lunch.

Is there a restaurant near here?

My grandma wants to buy cookies and milk.

Is there a supermarket near here?

My dad wants to put gas in the car.

Is there a gas station near here?

Pearson Education Limited
Edinburgh Gate
Harlow
Essex CM20 2JE
England
and Associated Companies throughout the world.

www.pearsonelt.com/bigenglish

© Pearson Education Limited 2015

Authorised adaptation from the United States edition entitled Big English, 1st Edition, by Mario Herrera and Christopher Sol Cruz. Published by Pearson Education Inc. © 2013 by Pearson Education, Inc.

The right of Mario Herrera and Christopher Sol Cruz to be identified as the authors of this Work have been asserted by them in accordance with the Copyright, Designs and Patents Act 1988.

First published 2015
Tenth impression 2026

ISBN: 978-1-4479-8931-8

Set in Heinemann Roman
Printed in Slovakia by Neografia

Acknowledgements

The publisher would like to thank the following for their kind permission to reproduce photographs:

(Key: b-bottom; c-centre; l-left; r-right; t-top)

123RF.com: captblack76 150 (b), Cathy Yeulet 100, Gilberto Mevi 118 (sandwich), Jacek Chabraszewski 28, Jasmin Merdan 27bl, jreika 155r, Lisa Young 12, lsaloni 155l, maxaltamor 42 (a), Nagy-Bagoly Ilona 13/3, Neven Milinković 69 (d), patrickhastings 154l, Pratchaya Leelapatchayanont 139t, romasph 121 (apple), Serhiy Kobyakov 152, tomwang 13/2, viewstock 101t, Virgilijus Norkus 29t; **Alamy Images:** ableimages 94c, 106/4 (centre), Aflo Co. Ltd 150 (d), Alex Segre 58/7, 69 (c), ARGO Images, Art Directors & TRIP 145/5 (2), 160/4 (right), Asia Images Group Pte Ltd 9r, 21br, 27br, 72r, 75bl, 95l, 113/3, 123bl, 140bl, 151, Bert de Ruiter, Blend Images 74/6, 81bl (pilot), Bob Masters 42 (d), BUILT Images 40, Cultura Creative (RF, Danita Delimont 30, David Young-Wolff, Denkou Images 88t, Easy Production 127/1, F1online digitale Bildagentur GmbH 70 (b), Gari Wyn Williams 73/1, Glow Asia RF Stickers (top right), Graham Oliver 58/11, Hemis 64 (d), Ian Dagnall 58/6, imagebroker 68 (b), Jeff Greenberg 4/4, 20/2, 21 (c), Joerg Boethling 46r, KidStock, Martin Wilson 150 (a), myLAM 150 (c), Nikreates 121 (carton of juice), Pawel Libera Images 42 (b), Purepix 31l, Radius Images, simon margetson travel 36br, 52/3 (left), Steve bly 85/3, Ted Foxx 48br, TomBham 58/5, uwe umstatter, VStock 29 (Jim), Zak Waters 86tr; **Corbis:** David Bathgate 15 (d), Jan Haas / dpa 70 (a), Bruce Laurance / Blend Images 1l, Margaret Courtney-Clarke 31r, SUPRI / X00477 / Reuters 47r; **Datacraft Co Ltd:** 70 (c); **DK Images:** Andy Crawford 96 (d), Britta Jaschinski 58/1, 106/1 (left), Cyril Laubscher 140/30 (parrot), Lorenzo Vecchia 122b, 123 (kiwi), Lucy Claxton, Martin Richardson (c) Rough Guides 64 (b), 128/8, 135/2, Max Alexander 73/2, Robert Holmes, Ruth Jenkinson 8/1, Simon Rawles 94b, 106/4 (right), Steve Gorton 16tr, 21 (b), 24 (skateboard), Tim Draper (c) Rough Guides 128/7, Tim Ridley 112/11, Vanessa Davies 4/8, 19/2, William Shaw 112/15, 124/5; **Eyewire:** 20/3, 35/2; **FLPA Images of Nature:** David Hosking 140/29 (d); **Fotolia.com:** abdue 36tr, Alexandra Karamyshev 50cr, Andres Rodriguez 145/5 (1), 160/4 (left), Andrey Bandurenko 37tr, 43/16 (2), apops 80/3, Atiketta Sangasaeng 81bl (table), Berna Şafoğlu 119 (can), clairecliz 59, Darla Hallmark 43/16 (7), dasharosato 64 (c), dekanaryas 101b, Eric Isselée 135/1, 140/30 (fox), f9photos 96 (a), fotoperle 20/4, 21 (d), George Dolgikh 89/40 (T), Giuseppe Porzani 58/2, 106/1 (centre), goodluz 74/5, 89/2, GoodMood Photo 51/3, 52/4 (centre), Ilike 4/2, Ivonne Wierink 62cr, 66/21 (4), 112/12, 160/1 (centre), Jakub Krechowicz 112/6, jjpixs 13/1, Jose Manuel Gelpi 43/16 (1), Juulijs 16t (centre right), Konovalov Pavel 67/3, krsmanovic 58/3, 106/1 (right), laszlolorik 66/21 (1), Lucky Dragon 32 (a), Lusoimages 50c, Maksim Shebeko 119 (oranges), matka_Wariatka 5t, Michael Ireland 32 (c), Michael Shake 43/16 (3), Monika Wisniewska 86cr, Monkey Business 32 (b), 119 (cookies), moodboard 156/3, Moreno Novello 14 (b), Morphart 43/16 (6), motorlka 112/5, 113 (c), 124/3, 160/1 (right), Natika 118 (crisps), Olga Sapegina 113tr, Pavel Losevsky 58/10, picsfive 118 (chocolate), 121 (chocolate), primopiano 112/13, 121 (burger), r-o-x-o-r 64 (a), Reflekcija 51/1, 52/4 (left), Rob, Robert Wilson 43/16 (5), RT Images 43/16 (8), 50tc, RTimages 20/1, 21 (a), 35/1, 52/2 (left), RusGri 112/14, 124/4, shock 58/8, shutswis 51/4, 52/4 (right), snaptitude Stickers (bottom left), stockphoto-graf 81bl (milk), sumnersgraphicsinc 50tr, sveta 50cl, thepoo 66t, Tom Wang Stickers (bottom right), tropper2000 124/6, twixx 50tl, Tyler Olson 74/11, 106/2 (right), Václav Hroch

8/2, 13t, vlorzor 143/6, windu 143/3, yanlev 20/7, 52/2 (right); **Getty Images:** Damir Spanic 74/1, David Page Photography 116/2, Diane Collins and Jordan Hollender 4/6, 19/4, 52/1 (right), elvira boix photography 83, Gage 15 (c), JUAN SILVA 48/3, Katy McDonnell 4/3, 8/4, 52/1 (centre), Kazumasa Yanai 37cl, 79/2, Rubberball / Mike Kemp 144; **Glow Images:** Imagemore, Ron Chapple 156/4; **Imagestate Media:** John Foxx Collection 149 (d); **MIXA Co., Ltd:** 149 (c); **Pearson Education:** 20 (background), 24 (basketball), 36-37, 58-59 (background image), 74-75, 79/3; **Pearson Education Ltd:** Studio 8 11br, 18r, 27tr, 43br, 63l, 65br, 66/21 (3), 75br, 81br, 95r, 97br, 119br, 123br, 129br, Sophie Bluy 82, Trevor Clifford 15br, Jules Selmes 4/9, 74/10, Stickers (top left), Naki Kouyioumtzis 58/4, Sozaijiten; **Secretariat of Tourism, Buenos Aires:** Julian W 138l; **Shutterstock.com:** Aaron Amat, Africa Studio 123 (avocado), Alexander Ryabintsev, Alexey Goosev 128/6, 160/2 (centre), Andre Blais 32 (d), Andrjuss 112/9, 121 (cheese), Andy Dean Photography 74/4, Apples Eyes Studio 86tl, artjazz 89/4, AVAVA 98, Blend Images 45bl, 75t, Bruce MacQueen 134/1, Bryan Solomon 118 (cookies), Carlos Neto 128/2, Chris Bence 119 (pizza), Chris Fourie 129cl, Chris Howey 68 (a), Chris Jenner 73/3, Christopher Jones 74/2, 106/2 (left), Christopher Kolaczan 134/4, clawan 154-155 (background), Cora Mueller 20/5, 52/2 (centre), Csaba Peterdi 20/6, 35/4, 156/1, cycreation, davegkugler 128/1, 140/29 (c), 160/2 (right), Dean Bertoncelj 80/2, Diane Garcia 85/2, Diego Cervo 13/4, 91t, Dirk Ercken 136, Dmitriy Shironosov 74/9, Dmitry Naumov 20/8, 156/2, Dudarev Mikhail, Eky Studio 4-5, 20-21, eurobanks 118 (carrots), Evgeny Karandaev, Gemenacom (bike, jacket, skates), Goodluz 80/1, Horiyan 121 (milk), Iakov Filimonov 128/5, Ian Rentoul 139b, idiz 128/3, 137, 160/2 (left), Iriana Shiyan 36bl, 52/3 (centre), irin k, Jacek Chabraszewski 116/3, 127/2, James Steidl 42 (c), Jiri Hera 118 (sweets), John Kasawa 37cr, 51/6, Jonmilnes 84, karen roach 73 (ruler), Karkas 44, 62cl, 67/2, 143/2, Kesu 149, Kitch Bain 16tl, kkammphoto008 47l, Kladej, Kokhanchikov 127/4, Kzenon 26tl, Leah-Anne Thompson 145/4 (T), Ledoct 89/3, Lisovskaya Natalia 66/21 (2), Ljupco Smokovski 112/7, 116/4, Lorraine Kourafas 94t, 106/4 (left), Lucky Business 19/3, lynnette 51/2, Mark Bonham 74/3, 106/2 (centre), Matthew Cole 140/30 (snake), mexrix 112/10, 113 (a), Mike Price 135/4, 140/30 (whale), Minerva Studio, Monkey Business Images 4/7, 9l, 18l, 21bl, 26bl, 27tl, 32bl, 32br, 37bl, 37br, 41l, 43cl, 43cr, 50bl, 50br, 65tl, 65tr, 79bl, 79br, 81tr, 85br, 89/1, 91bl, 91br, 107l, 107r, 113/2, 117r, 127/3, 129bl, 133l, 140br, 149bl, 149br, Morgan Lane Photography 4/5, 19/1, MShev 1cr, Natalia Siverina, Nate A 145/4 (B), Naypong 128/11, Nick Berrisford 134/2, Sergey Novikov 1cl, odze 112/3, 113 (b), 121 (strawberries), 160/1 (left), P72 121 (cookies), 124/2, Paleka, Panco, Pavel V Mukhin 143/4, Perig 24 (tree), Peter Wey, photobank.ch 86bl, photocell 112 (placemat), 121 (placemat), PhotoNAN 143/1, ppfoto13 143/5, Presniakov Oleksandr 96 (c), rickyd 128/9, riekephotos 48/2, Rob Marmion 26bc, 35/3, Rohit Seth 29 (Tim), 45c, 79/1, Ronald Summers 24 (football), 62r, 67/1, ruslanchik 119 (salad), Sam Strickler 138r, Sarunyu_foto, Senol Yaman 149 (a), SergiyN 5br, 15bl, 16br, 25r, 48bl, 63r, 81tl, 88b, 97tl, 113/1, 126l, 133r, Serhiy Kobyakov 4/1, 52/1 (left), Shawn Hempel 140/29 (a), sixninepixels 43/16 (4), 51/5, Skazka Grez 118 (apple), Slaven 86cl, Smit, sootra 113 (background), stefanolunardi 1r, Stephanie Frey 48/1, Steve Cukrov 89/40 (B), stockyimages 1c, Stu Porter 128/4, Supertrooper, Tatik22 67/4, Tatuasha, Tatyana Vyc 112/2, 124/1, Tischenko Irina 153, Tomas Loutocky 36tl, 52/3 (right), Tungphoto 37tl, Valentyn Volkov 112/8, 122t, Victor Shova 128/10, Viktar Malyshchyts 62l, 112/1, Visionsi 74/8, Vitaly Korovin 112/4, Vladimir Koletic 74/7, Volodymyr Goinyk 129 (glacier), Warren Goldswain 102, wavebreakmedia 8/3, Willyam Bradberry 134/3, 134-135 (background), worldswildlifewonders 129tr, YapAhock 128/12, 135/3, Yuri Arcurs 29 (Alex), 45br, 79/4, Zadiraka Evgenii 16t (centre left), Peter Zaharov 129cr, Zigroup-Creations 46l, zimmytws 26tr, ZouZou; **SuperStock:** Biosphoto 140/29 (b), Blend Images 5bl, 16bl, 25l, 41r, 72l, 85bl, 97tr, 117l, 126r, Corbis 145/5 (3), 160/4 (centre), DeAgostini 96 (b), Exactostock 26br, Yuri Arcurs Media / SuperFusion 116/1; **www.imagesource.com:** Nigel Riches 29 (Sarah), 45t, photolibrary.com 58/9, 86br

Cover images: *Front:* **Shutterstock.com:** Iakov Filimonov l, Dudarev Mikhail c, stockyimages r

All other images © Pearson Education

Every effort has been made to trace the copyright holders and we apologise in advance for any unintentional omissions. We would be pleased to insert the appropriate acknowledgement in any subsequent edition of this publication.

Illustrated by

Robin Boyer, Zaharias Papadopoulos (hyphen), Jose Rubio, Christos Skaltsas (hyphen), Julia Wolf.

Unit 1, page 9

Unit 2, page 25

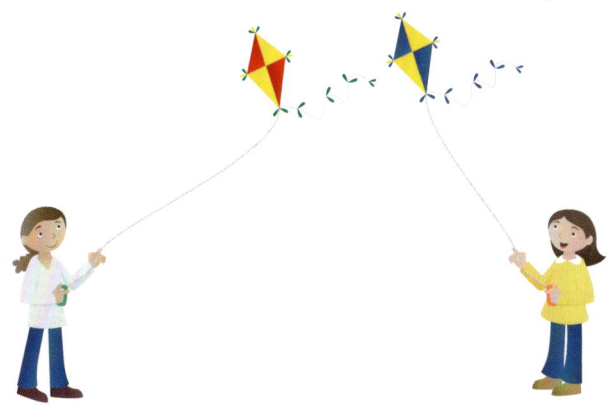  

Unit 3, page 41

Unit 4, page 63

Unit 5, page 79

Unit 6, page 95

Unit 7, page 117

Unit 8, page 133

Unit 9, page 149

June						
SUN	MON	TUE	WED	THU	FRI	SAT
					1	2
3	4	5	6	7	8	9
10	11	12	13	14	15	16
17	18	19	20	21	22	23
24	25	26	27	28	29	30

December						
SUN	MON	TUE	WED	THU	FRI	SAT
						1
2	3	4	5	6	7	8
9	10	11	12	13	14	15
16	17	18	19	20	21	22
23	24	25	26	27	28	29
30	31					

October						
SUN	MON	TUE	WED	THU	FRI	SAT
	1	2	3	4	5	6
7	8	9	10	11	12	13
14	15	16	17	18	19	20
21	22	23	24	25	26	27
28	29	30	31			

April						
SUN	MON	TUE	WED	THU	FRI	SAT
1	2	3	4	5	6	7
8	9	10	11	12	13	14
15	16	17	18	19	20	21
22	23	24	25	26	27	28
29	30					